T0049760

© Lauren R. Linehan/Krossel Kreek Photography

About the Author

Jenay Marontate began learning the secrets of kitchen witchery at an early age from her mother, grandmother, and great-grandmother. Now, she applies her knowledge of herbs, oil, magic, and kitchen witchery to her loose-leaf tea and spice business, Kitchen Witch Gourmet. Here, she infuses tea with magic, wellness, happiness, and love to brew the perfect cup. She also teaches tea leaf reading and other tea magic in the US and in China.

Tea Magic

Spells, Rituals, and Divination in Your Cup

JENAY MARONTATE

Llewellyn Publications ♦ Woodbury, Minnesota

Tea Magic: Spells, Rituals, and Divination in Your Cup © 2022 by Jenay Marontate. All rights reserved. No part of this book may be used or reproduced in any manner whatsoever, including internet usage, without written permission from Llewellyn Publications, except in the case of brief quotations embodied in critical articles and reviews.

FIRST EDITION
Second Printing, 2023

Book design by Mandie Brasington
Cover design by Kevin R. Brown
Interior illustrations by Llewellyn Art Department

Llewellyn Publications is a registered trademark of Llewellyn Worldwide Ltd.

Library of Congress Cataloging-in-Publication Data (Pending)
ISBN: 978-0-7387-6790-1

Llewellyn Worldwide Ltd. does not participate in, endorse, or have any authority or responsibility concerning private business transactions between our authors and the public.

All mail addressed to the author is forwarded but the publisher cannot, unless specifically instructed by the author, give out an address or phone number.

Any internet references contained in this work are current at publication time, but the publisher cannot guarantee that a specific location will continue to be maintained. Please refer to the publisher's website for links to authors' websites and other sources.

Llewellyn Publications
A Division of Llewellyn Worldwide Ltd.
2143 Wooddale Drive
Woodbury, MN 55125-2989
www.llewellyn.com

Printed in the United States of America

Contents

Legal Disclaimer

The information in this book is for educational purposes only. Please consult with your physician to make sure any teas or plants will not have an adverse side effect with any medications you may be taking.

It is advised that you also consult with an attorney in your area to counsel you about the laws and legalities surrounding the use of any plants, especially cannabis, in your county, state, and country.

To my mothers, grandmothers,
great grandmothers,
and the ones who came before.

Introduction

Images of witches with cauldrons and apothecaries of herbs and roots have filled the imagination of people for generations when they think of potions, spells, and healing elixirs through tea. For others when they think of tea, the magical aspects of it are not what initially come to mind. In this case, people are reminded of the beautifully elaborate tea ceremonies in China and Japan, or the traditions of teatime in the United Kingdom. Whereas for others when they think of tea, they are taken back to their childhood when they were first introduced to the taste, aroma, and healing effects of tea.

Whatever imagery and feelings toward tea magic you have right now, as you will soon discover, there is much more to tea witchery than you likely ever imagined. You will come away with a deeper respect, appreciation, and understanding of how to joyously weave together tea, magic, witchcraft, and alchemy into your own divination practices and that of your own tea witchery.

A Foundational Understanding

Tea witchery and kitchen witchery are not something I recommend anyone jump into without proper context and respect for the potency of the magic itself. Having a foundational understanding of the healing power and magical properties of tea is what makes tea witchery powerful, pleasurable, and just plain fun!

For example, you may feel inclined to skip ahead to a chapter you are fascinated with only to find that when you go to put what you learned into practical use, the results may turn out to be much less than what you expected. This is not to suggest every time you work with tea magic you will always get what you want. It does mean, however, that with a foundational understanding and deep respect for the magic itself, coupled with a joyous, curious, focused, and grounded approach, you will stack the odds of success and enjoyment in your favor.

The first time I considered tea as a magical herb was when I was reading *Encyclopedia of Magical Herbs* by Scott Cunningham in the early 1990s. Since then, I have been using tea and herbal infusions in a whole new way. I have gone on to learn and expand on correspondences to black tea, green tea, white tea, oolong teas, and herbal brews for magical uses in spells, charms, mojos, talismans, and potions, all of which you will learn about in the book.

Whether you are new to tea magic or are a well-initiated practitioner in tea witchery, the content, length, and order of the chapters are designed intentionally for you to get the most out of your experience with the material. While the chapters vary in length, all of them are packed full of tips, insights, wisdom, and step-by-step magical workings you can apply to your own form of tea witchery.

Not only can you quench your thirst with tea, but you can aid in healing your body, mind, and spirit. You can also use tea in spell work, charms, and potions, all of which will be detailed. I say all of this because this book will introduce you to a lot of new ideas and approaches for merging your tea with magic. Therefore, whether you are new to all of this or are well versed in tea witchery, the book will resonate with everyone differently.

A Deep Appreciation for Tea Witchery

Like tea, this book delivers a wide variety of benefits, along with a vast array of uses. I invite you to follow your inner guidance to engage with the chapters in *Tea Magic* as you feel called to. That said, the book is intentionally designed to be read from the introduction to the conclusion, where you will find an extensive directory of correspondences for tea and herbs.

To make the most out of what you just read, many chapters conclude with a section called Next Steps. This is a summary of the key points for that chapter, along with suggestions for everyday applications in your journey with tea, kitchen witchery, spirituality, divination, and wellness.

In whatever way you are inspired to journey with the book, I do encourage you to take time to sit with the magical practices you will discover. This means not only feeling into your own intentions on how to engage with the potent energy of tea magic, but also giving yourself permission to get creative with how to use tea in your expanded understanding of tea witchery.

No matter how much you know or do not know about tea witchery, my intention is that when you are finished with this book, you will come away with a greater awareness for how to use tea and tisanes as a powerful instrument with your own practices in divine magic and witchcraft. You will also have gained a deeper appreciation for how tea aids your mental, physical, emotional, and spiritual health.

I Am a Kitchen Witch

As a young girl and throughout my adult years, I have enjoyed a lifelong love affair with tea magic and kitchen witchery. It did not occur with expectations or involve far-flung dreams of authorship or even entrepreneurship. Like most love affairs, it happened when I least expected it, and unfolded in the most surprising and unexpected of ways.

My mom and I would forage for mint on my grandmother's property in Scoggins Valley, Oregon. She would say, "Wild mint grows everywhere the sun shines." We would take the mint back home and bundle the ends with yarn, hanging it up on the porch to dry. Once it dried, we would break off the leaves and lightly crumble them into old canning jars, storing it for later.

Mom was the hippy herbalist type, always reading up on natural remedies and Chinese medicines. She was always planting and plucking and engaged in herbal teamaking. She especially liked to grate ginger and lemon peel together. I was fascinated with how focused and yet how joyous and carefree she was.

Thankfully, my grandmother and great-grandmother both recognized my natural interest and keen instincts in kitchen witchery, although neither of them referred to it as kitchen witchery. Both would graciously allow me to shadow their movements in the garden and in the kitchen. Along the way, they would give me hands-on lessons working with herbs and natural remedies, while also gleefully offering up insights into the spiritual and metaphysical worlds.

Those were magical moments with my grandmothers in the garden and in the kitchen, but they weren't the only experiences gifted to me when it came to learning about tea witchery. For a young, energetic child who found it difficult to stay still, I managed to stay present while sitting on the porch or sofa listening to my mom share insights from the eclectic set of metaphysical books she was reading. Never did I imagine these wonderful, collective experiences as a child would someday lead me to forming my dream business, Kitchen Witch Gourmet, and writing my own book.

Since my business was birthed into the world, my life has positively changed in ways I could not have imagined. Through this journey, I have been blessed with numerous opportunities to share my love of tea magic and kitchen witchery with tens of thousands of tea drinkers from around the world. This includes the popular tea blends my team and I have concocted as well as teaching the mystery, history, magical practices, and healing benefits of tea magic at seminars and workshops across North America and even in China.

I do not share any of this to impress you but instead to provide you a good starting point for the magical journey we are taking together. Rest assured, nothing in this book is based on theory. Everything you will discover in *Tea Magic* is grounded in the proven workings of magic, steeped in real-world experiences, and supported by a long, rich, and colorful history of tea witchery, all of which makes tea magic so, well, magical!

A Gift from My Heart to Yours

There are many individual facets to tea magic, not to mention all that goes into the unlimited ways to weave them together. Therefore, it is almost impossible to become an expert overnight. I want to invite you to take everything you learn, one step at a time, especially if you are new to much of what you will discover. If you are advanced in the practices of tea witchery, you will know the pace you are most aligned with.

I could not have imagined the places my love affair with tea witchery would take me or the beautiful souls I would be introduced to through the business and teaching about tea magic and kitchen witchery. The fact that doing what I love and loving what I do would also lead to me writing a book on all of this is beyond my wildest dreams. None of this was planned. It manifested out of a lifelong love affair for all things magical.

The journey has not been easy, but I was guided by an uncompromising intention to honor the joy, love, and magic of tea, along with honoring the rich and colorful history of tea. These intentions are lovingly, magically, and deliberately woven into every chapter of this book, making this a gift from my heart to yours.

Chapter 1

What Is Tea Witchery?

Tea, tisanes, herbal concoctions, and magic potions have been with us for centuries. Many families have recipes dating back generations that have been applied to make one feel better, whether physically ill, heartbroken from a romance gone awry, or conjuring up spells for manifesting a heart's desires. Considering the modern reintroduction to the benefits and magical applications of tea, it is not surprising that many are rediscovering their grandmothers' and grandfathers' wisdom of herbs and natural medicines.

Just as a remarkable as the resurgence in tea is rising around the world, so too is the gaining popularity of tea witchery. As a result of my extensive travels teaching tea witchery and kitchen witchery, I am seeing tea more openly infused into a variety of magical practices. I also see this in the stories my customers share and observing the increasing number of posts on social media on these topics.

From spiritual ceremonies, meditation, and yoga, to what has become one of the more popular, modern practices with the creative and endlessly fun experiences of tea parties, tea witchery is catching on with a wide variety of people like never before. Of course, this is not a new fad, as today's modern-day love affair with tea witchery is a reflection of how tea has been enjoyed and practiced throughout the ages.

Although a lot of tea witchery takes place in the outer world, if you desire a specific outcome in your life, there is only one place to go that breathes your desire into reality: going within. When it comes to creating intimacy and magical outcomes with your tea, of all the ingredients and practices you can conjure up, visualizing what it is you desire is one of the most important.

Creating a Magical Life

There are many variations of techniques and processes for conjuring, visualizing, and manifesting your desires into existence through tea witchery, many of which I share in the forthcoming chapters. On some level, they all work but in my experience, there is no one technique or process that works the same for everyone. There are, however, three important ingredients for creating magic through tea witchery, no matter what practice you are called to engage in: embody the qualities of abundance of happiness, approach life with an open mind and curiosity, and trust the infallible guidance of your inner voice.

I believe having an abundance of happiness is the foundation to all things magical. When you embody happiness, things begin to grow, successes flourish, and the ideal people become magnetized to you. You are attracting abundance and joy to you because you feel good to be around. This aids in attracting the things you desire in life.

Happiness can move mountains; it can grow a business, a family, and friendship, and it can fill your life with magic and amazement. And remember, curiosity is one of the main ingredients to unlocking the magical properties and healing powers of tea magic and kitchen witchery.

For my own tea witchery practice, when it comes to listening to the infallible guidance of my inner voice, I have played around with different processes and visualization techniques, tweaking some and discarding others. This is always based on listening to the guidance of my inner voice, feeling into what is right at the time, and taking into careful consideration the specific nature of my desired outcomes.

Tea is Magic and Alchemy

When you get beyond the incredible taste and healing benefits of tea, and even go beyond the elegant pageantry of the ancient and current ceremonial rituals of tea, you discover what tea really is.

Tea is a blend of magic and alchemy. While there are different levels and perspectives of alchemy, just as there is with magic, when you are brewing tea, you are placing natural matter from the earth into boiling water to create a potion, a concoction, and a wellness remedy—all in one! Of course, this process is not like producing gold, but is it not alchemy in its purest essence?

When you infuse your intentions for drinking your tea into the tea itself, either consciously or unconsciously, you are weaving magical spells that fuse with and amplify the existing potency of the alchemy of tea. When you are consciously aware of these elements and practicing magic, the possibilities for enjoying more health, fun, abundance, romance, and joy in your life are endless!

The Kitchen Witch Legend

To deepen your understanding of tea magic and kitchen witchery while also getting the most out of this book's magic requires an understanding of both the legend and modern-day practice of kitchen witchery. We will start with the kitchen witch legend.

A kitchen witch is a doll or poppet that originated in Scandinavian countries many generations ago. These dolls were made to ward off bad luck and to keep your home safe, warm, and protected. A kitchen witch keeps a watchful eye over your meals so they do not burn. She also keeps harmony in your home and is always ready to make sure your cup of tea is absolutely perfect. These kitchen witch dolls were once handed down from mother to daughter and given to a bride to grace her new home.

Kitchen witches were traditionally hung in the kitchen near the stove, in a window, or in the entry to the kitchen. They were made of cloth and sticks and were generally featured as the old crone woman style-witch.

It is my intent to bring the legend of the kitchen witch into a new season by envisioning her as a fun, happy, and welcoming witch. She still holds the same duties as her grandmothers; after all, kitchen witchery runs in the family of witches. Only now she rides her broom with happiness and joy as she is out and about with a gracious wave and an uplifting hello.

Kitchen Witchery

Kitchen witchery, or kitchen magic, is a kind of magic that does not require fancy and rare herbs or tea supplies from far-off and exotic countries. If you are wondering how to get started with bringing tea magic to your everyday kitchen witchery, begin by looking through your current tea collection, as that is a great place to start.

Using tea and herbal infusions in magic has the benefit of being close at hand. Most people have some sort of tea in their cupboard. Herbal infusions are also a great resource to find herbs for magical work. For example, if you are out of plain chamomile, cut open a tea bag that contains chamomile and pick it out. If you are not an avid tea drinker, there are countless ways to order high-quality tea, from local supermarkets to online retailers.

Tea mixes, especially herbal ones, carry many ingredients to be used for magical purposes. If it is loose tea, pick out the specific herbs you need. If the tea comes in a bag, break it open and explore what is inside. Curiosity is one of the main ingredients to unlocking the magical properties and healing power of tea magic and kitchen witchery.

When it comes to infusing magic into your tea, brew, or potion, the process begins by using intent and clear focus with your desired outcome. This can be done by clearly stating your intent while you prepare your tea, brew, or potion. You can write your intent in the form of a spell, an incantation, or even prayer, to be spoken over the brew while it is steeping. This provides direction for the plants and activates their qualities for healing and imbuing.

By drinking in or imbuing the tea, you are taking the plant essences or plant magic into your body. This reflects the axiom "As above, so below; as within, so without." You have readied yourself and charged yourself with the will of the plants. You can now begin to manifest and create the changes you are seeking by becoming the infused and charged tool of intent and focused energy. In essence, you have become the magic, the power of will, and the living embodiment of your desire.

Respect the Power of Tea Witchery

I wrote this book because of my love and lifelong devotion to the multifaceted and multidimensional nature of tea witchery, a blend of both tea magic and kitchen witchery. Despite a level of mastery, which was attained with tea witchery over the course of several decades, I, respectfully, remain a humble student in working with tea magic's power. It is with this same level of respect that I invite you to approach your workings with tea witchery, no matter the level of experience you may already have.

Holistic health and wellness aids in healing the spirit, in addition to healing the physical body. Using the natural essence of tea and plant magic helps you connect with your spirit so you can manifest change within yourself, your environment, and the world you live in. By working with the healing and spiritual benefits that are associated with tea and herbs and respecting the power of magical practices, you can truly obtain health and balance in your body, mind, and spirit through tea witchery.

Without a healthy respect and grounded understanding of the power behind combining tea with magic, it is easy to lose touch with what is at the heart of tea witchery. It is many things, but above all, tea witchery is immensely joyful, fun, prosperous, romantic, and it delivers abundant health benefits. Now that you know what tea witchery is, to make the most of your experiences with tea witchery, it is beneficial to know the types of tea and how to brew them, which is the focus of the next chapter.

Chapter 2

Six Types of Tea and How to Brew Them

Next to water, tea is the second most consumed beverage in the entire world. Combine that with the growing popularity of tea magic and kitchen witchery, and it is not surprising that of all the questions I am asked, two of the most consistent are how many types of tea there are and how to brew them.

Contrary to what many people believe, there is only one plant that produces tea. *Camellia sinensis*, otherwise known as tea, is an evergreen shrub native to East Asia. It is from this plant that six distinct classes, or types of tea, come from.

Although there are hundreds of tea-growing regions all over the world that produce fine teas for their distinct qualities and profiles, these are the six that are the most common: white, green, yellow, black, oolong, and pu-erh. These six all contain caffeine. What makes them different, and what varies with the caffeine level, is the way they are cured, dried, and processed.

With so many tea-growing regions, there are also hundreds of brands of tea. The variations are vast, but for the purpose of our journey together with tea witchery, we will focus on the six types of tea, how to best brew them, and explore the magical applications, correspondences, and folk uses of these six teas.

White Tea

White tea is derived from the newly picked baby buds and two top leaves of the tea plant. The buds are so new that you can still see the fine, silvery white hairs glisten on the unopened buds, giving the tea a white appearance when picked. White tea is the least processed of the six types of tea.

A short steam or a quick fry in a pan is used to stop the oxidation of white tea before being dried and packaged. White tea contains the least amount of caffeine and the highest amounts of antioxidants. Lightest in flavor, the taste leans into light floral, grassy, and fruity notes. An essence of honey or sweetness are sometimes detected. The recommended water temperature is 160 to 170 degrees Fahrenheit. The steep time is ninety seconds to two minutes.

Magical Applications, Correspondences, and Folk Uses of White Tea

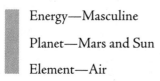

Energy—Masculine

Planet—Mars and Sun

Element—Air

White tea, which is sometimes called silver tips, is known for bringing joy, clear focus, clarity, enhancement of health, and emotional healing. It's also know for renewing skin and hair, delivering a healthy shine. White tea is a superior clear-thinking tea for meditation and prayer, which is why it is ideal for purifying your thoughts and actions and bringing blessings and protection.

For these reasons and more, magical applications, correspondences and folk uses of white tea include enhancing psychic ability, cleansing auras, balancing chakras, clear thinking, and connecting to the Divine, spirits, and deities.

Using white tea to cleanse magical tools helps to neutralize negativity and balance the tools' proper energy. You can also burn the leaves as an offering to deities and loved ones who have crossed over.

Green Tea

Green tea is the most common tea in Asia, as it was first grown there. Today, green tea is now grown in many countries. This tea comes from the leaves and buds of the *Camellia sinensis* plant that have been lightly processed. After being picked, the leaves are laid out to dry for a very short time. The leaves are then rolled to release moisture. Following that, the leaves are tossed onto a large wok-type pan and are quickly fried to release the remaining moisture and stop all oxidation before completing the drying cycle.

Green tea has more caffeine than white tea. It is rich in antioxidants. Green tea has a crisp flavor, can be herbaceous and buttery, and have undertones of grassy freshness and earthiness. This tea can become bitter if steeped too long. The recommended water temperature for green tea is 170 to 180 degrees Fahrenheit. Steep time is ninety seconds to two minutes. This tea may be steeped up to three times.

Magical Applications, Correspondences, and Folk Uses of Green Tea

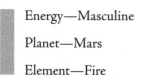

Energy—Masculine

Planet—Mars

Element—Fire

Magical applications, correspondences, and folk uses of green tea are quite vast. Green tea can aid in supporting your optimal health, promoting vitality, increasing energy and passion, aiding in alertness and focus, and supporting clear thinking. It also has ties to supporting luck, prosperity, and love.

Green tea delivers a deep connection to your body, mind, and spirit, making it a beneficial drink to have before meditation, as it enhances long periods of focus. Using green tea leaves in a mojo bag can act as a protection of health.

If all of these applications were not enough reasons for drinking green tea, this tea is also known to act as an anti-inflammatory, may boost the metabolism, improve brain function, regulate dopamine, and has been linked in helping to reduce the risk of stroke and heart failure. For these reasons and more, green tea builds and strengthens your will and is a fantastic tea for your overall well-being.

Yellow Tea

In relation to the previously mentioned teas, yellow tea has an additional step in when it is processed. The extra step comes after the quick frying, where the tea is placed in a dark wooded box to cool and allowed to oxidize very slowly. This process can last up to three days using careful control to reach the perfect oxidization. The process creates a yellow glow to the leaves. The last step is a final fry to release the remaining liquid and finalize the drying, producing yellowish, light brown tea.

Yellow tea is light in flavor, leaning to a slight vegetable taste, sometimes with citrus and earthy undertones. Its caffeine level is similar to green tea. The recommended water temperature to steep yellow tea is 170 to 180 degrees Fahrenheit. Steep time is ninety seconds to two minutes.

Magical Applications, Correspondences, and Folk Uses of Yellow Tea

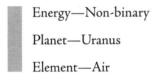

Energy—Non-binary

Planet—Uranus

Element—Air

Magical applications, correspondences, and folk uses of yellow tea may not be as far reaching as green tea but it delivers some highly sought-after benefits. With a lower caffeine level, yellow tea is not as overpowering as black tea or green tea but is quite uplifting.

Correspondences for yellow tea include happiness, prosperity, abundance, and health, which make it a wonderful tea for meditating on wellness and abundance. With its mild and crisp flavor profile, as well as being low in acid and tannins, yellow tea is easy on sensitive tummies.

Oolong Tea

Oolong tea is a tea that has been processed when the *Camellia sinensis* plant's growth is at its halfway point between green tea and black tea. This allows the tea to retain a number of benefits similar to green tea while also providing a richer, smoother flavor of a black tea.

Oolong tea follows the same process as black and green tea: picking the leaves, allowing the tea to wither, rolling it, giving it time to partially oxidize, and then frying and packaging it. Some of the differences between this tea and its counterparts, though, is that its process does not allow the leaves to fully oxidize. This ensures oolong tea has a full-bodied flavor and higher caffeine level similar to black tea but retains some of the health benefits and antioxidants found in green tea.

Oolong tea's flavors range from a toasty richness to earthy, nutty, and sometimes sweet undertones. The recommended water temperature is 180 to 200 degrees Fahrenheit. Steep time is ten seconds to one minute. It is traditional that this tea is steeped a few times, revealing layers of flavor being released from each steep. With each steep increase the time by ten to sixty seconds.

Magical Applications, Correspondences, and Folk Uses of Oolong Tea

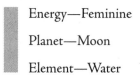

Energy—Feminine

Planet—Moon

Element—Water

Magical applications, correspondences, and folk uses of oolong tea include love, reflection, emotional balance, inner peace, and spiritual well-being. Because oolong tea is processed right between the growth stages of green tea and black tea, it lends itself to be a facilitator of balance, as it keeps you energized and focused but also producing a sense of calm.

For these reasons and more, there are many magical and folk uses for oolong tea. These include divination, meditation, balanced thinking, and bringing deep reflection on relationships and matters of the heart.

Oolong tea carries many health benefits as well and is known for promoting heart health, dental health, and skin health. Using oolong tea in love amulets strengthens attractions. The leaves can be burned with roses to enhance love.

Oolong is also regarded as a great promoter of truth. An old wives' tale claims that drinking oolong with your guest will reveal truths and may act as a truth serum in some situations.

Black Tea

Sometimes called red tea, black tea is the most common tea outside of Asia.[1] It is no surprise then that black tea is the most consumed tea in the United States and British markets.[2] This tea is produced in several countries around the world and is most often a blend of more than one tea from different regions. For instance, there is Assam black tea, which is the pride and joy of India.

Black tea consists of the same leaves and buds plucked from the *Camellia sinensis*. They are left to lie out for up to eighteen hours to wither. The length of time they are laid out causes their leaves' color to turn from green to reddish-brown. The tea is then rolled to release moisture, sometimes left to wither again, and then rolled again.

The next phase of processing black tea involves the tea being tossed onto a large hot surface to fry quickly, halting the oxidation. From there, the tea is then dried completely, which changes its color again to a darker shade of brown and black. From this point, the tea is packaged and shipped out.

Black tea contains more caffeine than its sister teas of green tea and white tea but a lower number of beneficial antioxidants. It is a full-bodied tea in terms of flavor, with a rich and earthy taste. Malty, smoky, spiced, caramel, and floral notes can be detected in many black teas. The recommended water temperature to steep black tea is 190 to 200 degrees Fahrenheit. Steep time is three to five minutes. Black tea may be steeped up to three times.

---

1. Pettigrew and Richardson, *The New Tea Companion*.
2. Ibid.

Magical Applications, Correspondences, and Folk Uses of Black Tea

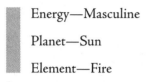

Energy—Masculine

Planet—Sun

Element—Fire

Magical applications, correspondences, and folk uses for black tea include productivity, protection, divination, spirit work, banishing, stability, power, and prosperity. Additional characteristics for black tea include courage, strength, riches, and enhancement of inner power.

Black tea is an ideal base for infusions—combining tea with other ingredients such as fruit or flowers. You can also burn the leaves of black tea during ceremonial practices to ensure future financial abundance.

Black tea can also be infused and woven into talismans with the intention to bless the bear with additional courage, strength, and confidence.

Assam black tea, which is from India, is a rich, hardy black tea. Its health benefits include prolonged stamina and clear focus, and may lower blood pressure and increase blood flow to vital organs such as the heart, liver, and lungs. This tea is also well known for boosting energy and stamina, while also aiding in lowering blood pressure. It may also promote bone density and dental health.

Pu-erh Tea

Pu-erh can be one of the most expensive teas in the world, depending on how long it is cured and aged before it hits the retail market.[3] This is due to the year of the crop, the storage of the tea, and the length of years it has been stored. Pu-erh tea is the only tea that is left to ferment over time. In fact, the longer it has aged, the more sought-after the tea.

Different lengths of fermentation times pull out different flavor profiles of the tea. The process starts the same as other teas, in that the tea is picked, then withered. It is then placed in controlled bins to ripen and ferment. This process may

---

3. Pettigrew and Richardson, *The New Tea Companion.*

take one or many years to perfect the desired flavor. Once it ferments the tea is steamed and pressed into cakes. This slows the fermentation process. However, it never completely stops.

Akin to wine, pu-erh ages well, and over time its deep, rich, and earthy flavors are enhanced. The taste is heavier than all other tea counterparts, with strong earth, deep molasses, spicy, and chocolaty notes bringing pu-erh teas to full rounded finishes. Pu-erh tea has caffeine levels similar to black tea. The recommended water temperature for steeping is 205 to 210 degrees Fahrenheit. Steep time is thirty seconds to one minute. It is traditional that pu-erh tea is steeped several times (up to ten times is acceptable), revealing layers of flavor released at each steep. Pu-erh is known as the slow tea, intended to be sipped and savored, enjoying all layers and complexities of the tea. With each steep, increase the time by twenty to sixty seconds.

Magical Applications, Correspondences, and Folk Uses of Pu-erh Tea

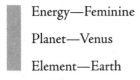

Energy—Feminine

Planet—Venus

Element—Earth

Magical applications, correspondences, and folk uses of pu-erh tea include clarity, alertness, romance, and wisdom. This tea is also useful when working on memory recall and may be used to understand family history. For this reason, pu-erh is an aid when blending past and future together.

Pu-erh is known to offer a myriad of health benefits. These may include supporting health while dealing with ailments such as diabetes or high cholesterol, and may increase stamina and fortitude.

Six Honorable Mentions

Although there are six primary types of tea, there are what I like to refer to as the six honorable mentions—variations of tea—that are favorites and go-to drinks for millions around the world.

Darjeeling Tea

Darjeeling is a black tea that that was established in the Darjeeling mountains of India. In a class of its own, Darjeeling tea is known as the "champagne of teas" and is revered for its flavor, vibrancy, and superiority. There are many layers to this delicate tea with crisp citrus notes and a floral finish.

Processing this tea yields white tea, green tea, and black tea. The process itself is much the same as a classic green tea in terms of picking the leaves, allowing them to wither, and then rolling and frying them. Where the difference comes in between this tea and the others is due to the climate of the Darjeeling mountains and the expertise of the plantation owners. Darjeeling tea has a high caffeine content, similar to black tea. The recommended water temperature 190 to 200 degrees Fahrenheit. Steep time is three to five minutes. This tea may be steeped up to three times.

Magical applications, correspondences, and folk uses for Darjeeling include health and vitality. It may also be a powerful aid when meditating on prosperity, wealth, and luxury.

Lapsang Souchong

Lapsang souchong is a black tea and is sometimes referred to as the "smoked tea." This is because the leaves are dyed in bamboo baskets over a smoky pine fire. The fire leaves behind a robust, smoked flavor and a spicy, smooth richness. Lapsang souchong is a full-bodied tea with deep undertones of forest and flame. Lapsang has a high caffeine content. The recommended water temperature to steep it is 190 to 200 degrees Fahrenheit. Steep time is three to five minutes. This tea may be steeped up to three times.

Magical applications, correspondences, and folk uses for lapsang souchong include bringing balance and peace to war. This is often attributed to how it brings warmth and fire into the body, allowing oneself to become one with fire and tea.

Matcha

Matcha is a green tea that has been ground down to a fine, bright green powder. The powder is then whisked into hot water until it creates a frothy broth. This is traditionally how the Japanese began to prepare tea and how it became a central part of Japanese tea ceremonies.

Of all the teas, matcha is highest in antioxidants because the tea is ground so fine. Because of this, matcha tea makes its way directly into your blood stream, helping to boost wellness.

Matcha's flavor profile is a bit stronger than green tea but similar. It carries fresh citrus notes, grassy richness, and floral undertones. This preparation of green tea contains caffeine. The recommended water temperature is 170 to 180 degrees Fahrenheit. Matcha tea is not steeped. Instead, it is whisked with water, creating a frothy broth.

Magical applications, correspondences, and folk uses for matcha tea range from the spiritual to the physical. For instance, matcha has been known for centuries to help with inducing trance-like states of deep meditation, as it was originally used for this purpose by Buddhist monks. Matcha delivers great benefits to your health, promoting vitality and strength. It is also applied to magical practices and ceremonies for manifesting prosperity.

Herbal Infusions

Of all the misconceptions about tea magic, the most common is the belief that herbal teas are tea. Herbal teas are not tea. They have been lumped into the category because of the steeping method to extract flavor and beneficial properties. They are properly called *herbal infusions* or *tisanes*, and they contain no caffeine. They range from any type of flower, herb, root, bark, or leaf that is steeped and drank.

Over many centuries, we have been shown the importance and impact tea has had, and continues to have, on people all over the world. In our greater understanding of tea, and the wildly fascinating ways in which it is cultivated, used, and consumed, we can begin to witness the magic of tea witchery unfold.

Rooibos

Rooibos (pronounced "roy-boss") is an herb native to South Africa. Dutch settlers of South Africa popularized the brewing of rooibos in the 1700s as an alternative to the more expensive imported black tea of the time.[4] Rooibos is harvested, processed, and prepared like a true tea but is not *Camellia sinensis* proper. It is described as sweet, smoky, woodsy, caramel, vanilla, and earthy. Often called

---

4. Klipopmekaar, "The History of Rooibos Tea."

South African red tea, this herb contains no caffeine. The recommended water temperature is 200 to 212 degrees Fahrenheit. Steep time for rooibos is three to five minutes.

Yerba Maté

Yerba maté is an herb native to South America and is used to make the national drink of Argentina, Paraguay, Uruguay, and southern Brazil. Though this is not a tea in the traditional sense, it has a strong tea-like drinking culture related to it. Yerba maté is now sold in the global tea market as loose tea and in tea bags.

Yerba maté leaves do contain two times as much caffeine as black tea and can act as a stimulant. It does, however, contain less caffeine than coffee. Yerba maté is less acidic than tea or coffee, so it can be easier on the digestive system. The recommended water temperature for steeping is 170 to 180 degrees Fahrenheit.

Traditionally, yerba maté leaves are left in the cup and water is continuously added to the drink.

Magical applications, correspondences, and folk uses for yerba maté include boosting one's confidence and courage, along with increasing ambition, both mentally and physically. Yerba maté is also well known for boosting metabolism, helping burn belly fat, increasing physical energy, and aiding in overall wellness. It is also helpful in keeping you focused and alert.

Steeping Times

Each tea has recommended industry standards of water temperature and steeping times. As a rule of thumb, most teas respond best with really hot water, just under boiling point. If you pour boiling water over green, white, or yellow tea, it will scorch the leaves and the tea will taste bitter.

Black tea can handle boiling water, and most herbal blends can too. The mint family releases the best aroma under a boil. Harder things such as dried ginger, cinnamon, and orange peel all thrive under boiling water. On the other hand, flower petals prefer just under boiling to release their more delicate aromas.

Chai tea, also known as masala tea, which is black tea and hard spices, does well starting out in a boiling water to break down the cinnamon, ginger, and cardamom. This lends to the thickness and texture of the drink. It is also known to be able to steep for hours. This tea blend traditionally has milk added.

Importance of Water

Next to the quality of the tea leaves, water is the second most important element to making a cup of tea. In the United States, tap water is easily in our reach, and in most places, it is safe to drink. Tap water, however, does not necessarily make the best cup of tea.

The quality of tap water is going to depend on the source and how it is distributed. For example, some regions of the country have hard water that is high in minerals and sediments. This is usually followed by a high chlorine content aimed at breaking down the sediments and neutralizing any harmful bacteria that might be in the public water systems. Making a fine cup of delicate white tea could be overpowered by a heavy chlorine taste, which all but eliminates flavor and essence of the tea itself.

Using water that has been properly filtered, or high-quality bottled water, to make your tea allows the true flavor of the tea to shine through and delivers the healthy benefits and magical elements of your tea in its purest essence. Just as a poor water source can turn a superior tea into something not so desirable, using good quality water can transform a not-so-great tea to something healthy and tasty.

A good water source that is properly pH balanced is good for whatever you are brewing up, be it tea, coffee, or anything else. The easiest and most cost-effective way to ensure a great cup of tea is to install a water filtration system in your faucet. Until then, bottled water is fine.

Measuring Your Tea

Brewing a teapot or a cup of tea is an intuitive experience. Each leaf and blend varies in flavor and each person's taste preference varies too. The easiest thing to remember is "A teaspoon got its name for a reason." With that in mind, a teaspoon of loose tea should make an eight- to twelve-ounce cup of tea.

If you are a person who likes a strong robust sensation, however, you may want to add more tea. Steeping tea longer can also make the tea stronger, but sometimes it can also make the tea bitter. The variations of this depend on the type of tea.

If you are making a thirty-two-ounce pot of tea using a teaspoon per eight ounces, that would equal one tablespoon plus one teaspoon of tea for the teapot.

Dry Measurements Conversion Chart

3 teaspoons	1 tablespoon	¹⁄₁₆ cup
6 teaspoons	2 tablespoons	⅛ cup
12 teaspoons	4 tablespoons	¼ cup
24 teaspoons	8 tablespoons	½ cup
36 teaspoons	12 tablespoons	¾ cup
48 teaspoons	16 tablespoons	1 cup

Liquid Measurements Conversion Chart

8 fluid ounces	1 cup	½ pint	¼ quart	
16 fluid ounces	2 cups	1 pint	½ quart	
32 fluid ounces	4 cups	2 pints	1 quart	¼ gallon
128 fluid ounces	16 cups	8 pints	4 quarts	1 gallon

Preparing Sun Tea

Sun tea is a method of brewing tea by using the sun as your heat source. It is most often served over ice. Sun tea works best in a glass container, with a one-gallon or 3.78-liter glass jar being most ideal. The amount of tea can vary with taste preferences. If you are using tea bags, use about about two to three bags per liter. For a gallon of water, add seven tea bags. If you are using a large steeping ball, add two to three tablespoons of loose tea.

To prepare sun tea, fill a container with water and place the tea in, setting it outside in direct sunlight for two to four hours. There is a bit of an art form to this, as many sun tea lovers will attest to, so check and stir your tea periodically to test its taste and color.

If you are a fan of sweet tea, add the sugar when you add the water. This way the sugar will dissolve while in the sun.

Sun tea is perfect over ice or placed in the refrigerator for later. In fact, iced tea has become an American favorite. Originally invented in 1904, iced tea was introduced to a larger public market and popularized at the World's Fair in St. Louis, Missouri. Richard Blechynden, who was an American merchant, was sampling and selling hot tea, but due to a very unexpected hot summer's day at the World's Fair, customers were not interested in trying his tea. Richard then cleverly poured the tea over ice, and it immediately became a huge hit.[5] Today, iced tea is a staple for millions of Americans year-round.

How to Steep Tea

Like me, your love affair with tea may have unfolded in this lifetime, but the world's love affair with tea goes back thousands of years. It is a love affair that originated in China and then migrated to Japan, where new and more elaborate ways to engage in tea's myriad of health benefits were established. In fact, had it not been for a select group of Japanese Buddhist monks falling in love with tea during their sacred journeys to China, it is possible the world would not have been introduced to tea for thousands of more years. And certainly, the world would not have been introduced to matcha tea.

---

5. "Iced Tea History," What's Cooking America.

Although there is not an exact date of the original discovery of tea, the legend most agreed upon is that tea was discovered by Emperor Shen Nung, whose reign of China dates to 2737–2697 BC.[6] Tea bags, however, did not come into existence until the early 1900s.

How and where did the tea bag originate? Well, there are many myths and legends as to who invented the tea bag. However, the first patent of a mesh tea-steeping apparatus can be traced back to 1897. Over the next twenty years, this would morph and change into the easiest and most convenient way to brew tea.[7]

Since the late 1920s, tea bags became the acceptable way to brew tea. Today, when I share this history with people at seminars and workshops, most are surprised to learn that for much of tea's rich history over its first 6,000 years, tea bags were non-existent.

Despite the popular use of tea bags, the original way of infusing the tea into water was by adding loose-leaf tea right into the pot. This is a method still widely used today. In fact, it is the primary way most of my customers prefer to buy their tea.

For myself, I am partial to loose-leaf tea and loose herbal concoctions. I prefer this method because the quality of the tea and herbs are almost always fresher and a higher quality than those of pre-bagged tea and tisanes. When at home or when possible, I can custom blend my loose teas and tisanes to suite my taste, my meditation, or my magical workings.

I do, however, recognize that using pre-bagged teas are very convenient. I get it—there is zero fuss and no mess, and it serves those who are simply looking for convenient teatime enjoyment. I honor everyone's choices in how they prefer to receive, brew, and enjoy their tea. With that in mind, here are some additional methods for steeping your tea:

A Strainer

Using a strainer that fits over the top of your cup or pot is a perfect way to avoid excessively steeping your tea. It also allows you to extract the layers of aroma and flavors one pour at a time.

---

6. Zak, *20,000 Secrets of Tea.*
7. Richardson, "Boston Tea Party Ships and Museum."

Metal Tea Balls and Teaspoons

There are metal tea balls and teaspoons that have a mesh basket to put the tea in to allow water to flow through it, extracting the tea but keeping most of the leaves out of the water. These are easy to use for a cup of tea or a pot and are easy to clean.

Silicone Tea Infuser

Using a tea infuser made of silicone can add a bit of whimsy to your tea because they often come in fun shapes like dolphins, flowers, or whatever is trending. These are best for brewing green and white tea because there is no metal to retain excess heat on the leaves that can sometimes scorch the tea leaves or cause bitterness.

French Presses

French presses and infuser pots make great tea, especially if you like a stronger flavor. Being that the leaves stay in the water, they will release more flavor and tannins, creating a stronger and more robust cup of tea. Leaving tea leaves too long in water will also bring a bitterness.

Fill Your Own Tea Bags

There are fill-your-own tea bags on the market—disposable and reusable ones. These are easy and make convenient cups of tea on the go.

Ultimately there are many fun tea accessories and steeping tools. That is the fun part about being a tea drinker: you get to find what works for you and enjoy the journey of figuring out what you like one cup at a time.

Next Steps

Did you discover something new about tea by reading this chapter that has you even more excited about tea magic? Take some time to allow this new information, even if it is a nice refresher for you, to integrate and percolate. Also, be sure to go back through and review areas you want to brush up on and get a little more acclimated to.

For example, now that you have expanded your awareness of the six teas, how to brew them, and their correspondences and magical qualities, you may also be feeling called to engage in different types of teas with your magical practices. Then, there are the honorable mention teas, which you may be inclined to try if you have not already done so.

Whatever resonated with you the most, one thing we can all agree on is that the six teas, and even the honorable mentions, deliver a wide variety of tasty enjoyment, magical healing properties, and potent health benefits, just to name a few of the seemingly endless ways you can partake in a cup of tea.

In whatever ways you feel inspired to practice tea magic and engage in the art of kitchen witchery, you are likely doing so because you know the tangible benefits tea delivers to your mental, emotional, physical, and overall spiritual health and how it can also do the same for your family, friends, and clients.

I invite you to journey with me into the next chapter as we take a deeper exploration into learning some amazing facts about the incredible health benefits of tea.

Chapter 3

Powerful Health Benefits Of Tea

Over the years I have learned from countless people I have spoken with about tea and kitchen witchery that their initial experiences with both were the result of their mothers and grandmothers introducing them to it. This confirmed what I had not only experienced personally but also what I had learned through my research, which is that the powerful health benefits of tea have been an essential part of generational wisdom sharing.

There is power in kitchen witchery and healing potions that have been carried down from generation to generation. It used to be that our ancestors would go to the herb garden and pick fresh mint and brew a cup of tea if you had a tummy ache, or chamomile if you needed something more relaxing and easier on the nerves.

While there are six primary types of teas, as you just learned about, not all teas are equal in their health benefits. For this chapter, I will primarily focus on two of the most prominent and powerfully healing teas: green tea and Earl Grey (a type of black tea). You will also come to better understand the powerful health benefits of tea on a general level and apply these benefits to your enjoyment of tea, such as its use with meditating and aromatherapy.

If you are an avid tea drinker or well steeped in the practice of magic and kitchen witchery, this chapter presents an opportunity to refresh your already deep knowledge of the powerful health benefits of tea, specifically green tea and Earl Grey.

We will begin with the foundation of tea, which is water.

Healing Power of Water

When brewing a magical cup of tea, there are plenty of layers and elements to consider, not only for taste but also for your overall well-being. The first, if not the most important, is the water you choose. Clean pure water is the best to enhance and bring out the subtleties of the tea's flavors and color.

The healing power of water is so vast and significant to tea witchery there is no way to do justice to it with this brief introduction. Yet, it is essential to understand on a basic level when speaking to the health benefits of tea. Therefore, I devoted an entire chapter to water and its beneficial relation to tea magic, which expands on what I am sharing with you here.

Water steeps the essence and goodness of the tea leaves into a liquid state, which allows the benefits of tea to be carried into your body with water. Water is the carrier of the health benefits of tea, as it delivers nutrients to your blood and vital organs, and brings oxygen to your brain. When drinking tea, you are not only providing your body with its basic essential fluid for functioning, but you are also carrying with it the extraordinary benefits of tea via the sacred element of water.

Amazing Facts about Tea

Tea has been touted as the wonder tonic by many cultures for centuries. Many of those reasons can be attributed to green tea, which has a long history of health benefits. Now, with advanced modern technology, we can break the structure of tea down and explain what it is about tea that has earned it this reputation for a wide variety of incredible health benefits.

According to the National Cancer Institute, green tea's polyphenols are a powerful antioxidant reputed to be two hundred times stronger than vitamin E at reducing free radical damage, which slows the aging process of your cells.[8] Green tea has anticancer properties that protect the cells from carcinogens and toxins, and help to keep radioactive strontium out of your bones. This makes green tea an ideal drink for individuals undergoing chemotherapy.[9]

The chemicals found in green tea called *catechins* are antibacterial and antiviral. This means that they help to fight dangerous bacteria and viruses in the body that can cause illness. Catechins balance the good and bad bacteria in your gut, organs, and blood. This builds the immune system, helping to prevent colds, flu, and viruses.[10]

Green tea also has anti-inflammatory properties, which help reduce pain caused by swelling and inflammation. In addition to this, green tea has shown to be effective at lowering high blood pressure and is said to stimulate health function in the heart that may help prevent cardiovascular disease.[11]

Green tea may also help with respiratory problems because it is a bronchial dilator and mild decongestant. This helps ease asthma and breathing difficulties by increasing air flow to the lungs, which in turn provide oxygen to the brain.[12]

One of the biggest health benefit claims of green tea is that it helps you lose weight. It does this by helping to regulate blood sugar, reducing sugar and carb cravings. Green tea also helps to metabolize fat because the caffeine and the catechins in green tea combined can speed up the metabolism and increase energy, helping to break down excess fat faster.[13]

Black tea, oolong, and white tea also contain many of the same extraordinary health benefits of green tea. The difference is that these other teas are not as powerful as green tea. For example, when black tea is fermented and sweated to oxidize the leaves and create a much richer flavor, darker color, and bolder taste, the leaves loose some of their antioxidants and catechins.

---

8. "Tea and Cancer Prevention," National Cancer Institute.

9. Ware, "What Are the Benefits of Green Tea?"

10. "Tea and Cancer Prevention," National Cancer Institute.

11. Ohisi et al, "Anti-inflammatory Actions of Green Tea."

12. Zak, *20,000 Secrets of Tea*; Hartley et al, "Green and Black Tea for the Primary Prevention of Cardiovascular Disease."

13. Kandola, "Does Green Tea Help Weight Loss?" Medical News Today.

As for white tea, it is a very young tea and has not quite developed all the health properties as its big sister green tea. Though many benefits remain in the black and white tea family, they are just a little stronger in green tea, making green tea your go-to for a truly amazing partner in your efforts to get healthier and sustain that good health.

How to Meditate with Tea

Over the ages, meditation has undergone various definitions as it is many different things to different people. For me, meditation is the practice of quieting the inner chatter of the mind to welcome a relaxing, calm, and peaceful inner state of being. How to reach that point can be arrived at in a myriad of ways.

Meditation can occur through mindfulness and focused thought on a particular object, or an activity to gain an expanded awareness to achieve a mentally clear and emotionally stable state of being. Some practices require total silence to achieve optimum meditative outcomes. Other practices of being in nature, listening to music, guided meditation, or even a repetitive white noise like a fan, are helpful. Some practitioners can enter a meditative state in what would seem unlikely places such as public transportation, noisy and cluttered rooms, or sitting on a public bench in a crowded and hectic space.

Thousands of years ago, Buddhist monks were known for incorporating green tea into their deep, meditative sessions. They found green tea to help them sustain a clear and focused mind while enhancing longevity of their meditation practices.[14] All these years later, green tea is still a perfect cup of tea to meditate with, as it lends itself to increased focus, abundant health, and overall vitality.

In the last few decades, aromatherapy has grown in popularity as it has proven to be helpful with meditation, not to mention a host of other health benefits. With herbal infused teas, and specific blends with a powerful, healthy aroma, you have a trifecta of benefits with tea magic, aromatherapy, and meditation.

The one thing many people can agree on is that meditation is not easy, at least when you are first starting out. For many people, they find meditation boring and are unable to detach from the rapid and repetitive racing thoughts of their mind.

---

14. Pettigrew and Richardson. *The New Tea Companion.*

This was me early on in my life when I first tried meditation. Since then, I have discovered a process that delivers ease, clarity, and healthy benefits to blending tea with meditation.

Here are some simple and easy steps to weave into your tea and meditation practice:

+ Choose and make a cup of tea or herbal infusion for its aromatherapy benefits.

+ Focus your attention on a specific sound, or a single point of focus. After a few minutes, the mind will begin to settle down and the inner state of relaxation will become easier to welcome in.

+ Use a teacup as a focus point in meditation to give you something physical to hold, feel, and focus on. It is best to have just poured hot water into the teacup to allow your tea to steep for a few minutes.

+ Hold the teacup in your hand or simply set it on a table, allowing the steam to rise to you. Closing your eyes and inhaling the steam of the steeped herb can help set your mind on a focused path.

+ While the fragrance of the steam is being inhaled through the nose, take in the aromatherapy benefits to boost mental energy, clear the respiratory tract, alleviate feelings of nervous tension and stress, and soothe feelings of irritability.

+ When you exhale through the mouth, imagine blowing away all the obstacles in your way, such as any chaos or negative issues. This deep breathing cycle and inhalation of aromatherapy and tea can help you create balanced thoughts and welcome clarity. If this is new for you, start with a few deep breaths and work your way up to a few minutes and then longer.

+ From there, enjoy your tea and then focus on the completion of your daily tasks.

In whatever way you feel works best for you, having a teacup as a meditation tool can be helpful, both for beginning meditators and those who have been practicing for years. Some people find that chanting, saying affirmations, or speaking mantras prove to be additionally helpful while inhaling the steam from your cup. In doing this, I recommend keeping whatever you are speaking simple, as in one thought, phrase, or sentence.

This simple teacup meditation can be performed with any cup of tea. All you must do is start. It might take a little bit of time to create a focus, but the benefits are well worth the time and practice. Besides, you get a reward of a delicious cup of tea or herbal infusion at the end.

Just like that, not only have you learned to meditate but you are receiving the benefits of plant medicine, tea magic, and aromatherapy all in your cup of tea.

Healing Magic of Earl Grey

One of the world's most famous teas is Earl Grey, and it is not your average black tea. It is a black tea that is blended with bergamot essential oil, making it one of the more powerfully healing teas, alongside green tea. You can find Earl Grey tea just about anywhere tea is sold. It is easy to come by, easy to prepare, and perfect for infusing into many of your health or creative activities.

Black tea carries health benefits, such as antioxidants, that may help to regulate blood pressure, easing feelings of tension.[15] Also, tea is an anti-inflammatory, which helps reduce pain caused by swelling and inflammation.[16] The star ingredient in Earl Grey, though, is bergamot.

Bergamot is a citrus-related fruit indigenous to the Asian continent. The essential oils from the peel of this fruit are extracted then sprayed or perfumed over the tea leaves. Bergamot is highly touted and recognized as an essential oil with mood stabilizing effects.[17] Bergamot has been shown to relieve anxiety, ease restless thoughts, and promote cheerfulness, all of which help to uplift depressive states of the mind.[18]

Bergamot oil contains limonene and alpha-Pinene components, which act as natural sedatives and mood stabilizers. This is a great remedy for long stressful

---

15. Warner, "Drinking Black Tea May Soothe Stress." WebMD.

16. Tomokazan et al, "Anti-inflammatory Actions of Green Tea."

17. Zak, 20,000 Secrets of Tea.

18. Zieilinski, "Nine Benefits of Bergamot Essential Oil."

days because tea also contains flavonoids which reduce stress, anxiety, and nervous tension.[19]

The beautiful, uplifting scent and aromatherapy benefits of bergamot have been found to improve the mood, calm headaches, and ease tension.

Five Ways to Enjoy Earl Grey Tea

With all its healing benefits, it is not surprising that Earl Grey tea is an excellent way to blend tea, aromatherapy, and plant medicine all in one cup. Inhaling the rich scent of tea and the uplifting burst of bergamot can help with focus, clear thinking, and can act as a mood elevator.[20] Like any tea, Earl Grey has a variety of blends and ways to enjoy it.

Here are five popular ways Earl Grey tea is enjoyed, along with additional health benefits and magical properties.

Lady Grey

Lady Grey has the same base of black tea as the traditional Earl Grey tea, and it also is perfumed with bergamot. What makes Lady Grey unique among the Earl Grey blends is that it carries a much more subtle infusion of the citrusy flavor. This leaves Lady Grey lighter to taste with a milder flower and citrus flavor than your classic black tea.

Light and subtle, Lady Grey tea is great for handling delicate situations, such as those that require manors, etiquette, and grace. Lady Grey tea can be used to make someone feel welcome and comfortable while you slyly engage them in conversation in which you hope to glean knowledge or information from them.

Russian Earl Grey

In Russia, tea is a must following a meal. This is the time to socialize and relax, which is where a signature favorite tea comes into play: Russian Earl Grey. This tea has a black tea base that is heavily blended with citrus peels and lemongrass, giving the classic Earl Grey a run for its money in the robust flower, citrus flavor profile.

---

19. Nagdeve, "Ten Benefits of Bergamot Oil." Organic Facts; Paddock, "Does a Cup of Tea Reduce Stress?"
20. Nagdeve, "Ten Benefits of Bergamot Oil."

Russian Earl Grey sometimes starts with a black tea Earl Grey base, then the orange, lemon, bergamot, and lemongrass is added. With the abundance of citrus in Russian Earl Grey, the tea makes a perfect cup of aromatherapeutic meditation tea that is centered around rejuvenation, happiness, joy, and abundance. Russian Earl Grey is a tea of power and persuasion, thus, drinking this tea lends you access to big inspirations and grand ideas.

This tea is associated with masculinity, boldness, drive, and power. Therefore, Russian Earl Grey is an ideal tea to share when you are trying to get an idea across or trying to change the minds of your colleagues in a graceful and elegant manner.

Lavender Earl Grey

As the name suggests, this is a blend of Earl Grey tea with lavender. This blend gives an extra floral boost to the classic citrus of the Earl Grey, giving it a very heady and perfumed presence with the rich smoothness of black tea.

By adding lavender to this already naturally mood-stabilizing tea, you create an extra layer of relaxation and harmony. Lavender Earl Grey is a great stress-reducing tea blend that leaves you calm and clear minded. Using Lavender Earl Grey tea to meditate helps deliver laser-like clarity as it calms racing thoughts and relinquishes anxiety. This tea blend will also help soothe the side effects of being mentally and emotionally attacked. Because of this, Lavender Earl Grey is an excellent tea to engage with when you feel your psychic energy drained.

Earl Grey with Rose

Sometimes referred to as French Earl Grey, this blend of Earl Grey embodies the softer romantic notes of roses. Paired with the bold flavor of citrus in the bergamot, Earl Grey with rose produces a well-balanced flavor profile with just the right touch of romance.

Adding rose to Earl Grey evokes an element of love and beauty to your cup. This tea combines masculine and feminine elements and can be used to seduce a potential lover when shared together at dusk. Earl Grey with rose can also be a comforting and soothing cup of tea to share with a friend to help them ease heartache or understand a breakup.

As a Tea Witch, I believe that a cup of Earl Grey with rose can help soothe a broken heart, and ease the tension and stress of a breakup. I recommend this tea when all matters of the heart need to be soothed.

Jasmine Earl Grey

Combining two of the world's most popular perfumed teas, the jasmine Earl Grey tea blend is sometimes referred to as the lover's blend. With the addition of jasmine, this tea creates a beautiful, exotic, and desirable blend that can leave you in a state of tranquility and harmony.

Jasmine Earl Grey is a tea that holds the key to balance and spiritual awakening. For this reason, it is useful for helping unlock myths and mysteries. Jasmine Earl Grey is also a popular tea for helping facilitate group harmony and open deeper conversations when shared at tea parties and other gatherings.

Putting It All to Use

Drinking tea for your health is gaining in popularity as this new resurgence in tea rises. Because of this, all around the world people are recalling their grandmothers' and grandfathers' wisdom of herbs and natural medicines as they are infused into a cup of tea and prescribed for better health in the name of kitchen witchery.

Whether you are new to the health benefits of tea or you have been on the leading edge of using and sharing the powerful health benefits of tea with your family, friends, and even clients, what you have been introduced to in this chapter is just the beginning of all the ways you can vastly improve your health with the help of tea. For your next steps, I invite you to re-read this chapter to reacclimate yourself with some of the practices and to find which tea blends work best for you. From there, go and joyously put them to use in your life.

Also, this goes without saying, if you are experiencing any health issues, be sure to consult your doctor. Also, when it comes to the use of water in your tea, I highly recommend you use clean, filtered water.

Along with the health benefits of tea and its myriad of uses in spirituality, there are also limitless ways in which tea can be woven into divination and magical workings. This is important to consider as we conclude this chapter because when you are feeling good, you create a receptive field of energy to attract good things. As you continue further into your own workings of tea witchery, you will come to see how important your health is for creating the desired outcomes in your practices. And nothing is as beneficial to a good healthy cup of tea, or to your overall health, as water, which is the focus of the next chapter.

Chapter 4

The Magic and Power of Water

I love water. Born under a full moon, and having been raised in the Pacific Northwest, you could say I was predestined to love water. I have always been a bit puzzled at why others do not have a deep affinity for all things water, even though, without water, there is absolutely zero life on earth. In my observances, most people seem to take water for granted. Water is, after all, what we are, with our bodies being made up of 60 percent water and Mother Earth, herself, made of 71 percent water.[21] Water is the only substance on earth that can be a solid, liquid, or gas. Not only can water be in all three states, it can be in all three states at once. This is called a triple point. For all these reasons and more, I have always referred to water as the Vital Fluid.

I had some of the most fun writing this chapter compared to developing material for anything else in the book. So, it should come as no surprise to anyone that a book based on tea witchery is incomplete without at least one chapter dedicated to the foundation of tea—water!

What you will discover in this chapter are the different types of water, the power of rainwater, rain's metaphysical and healing correspondences, which days of the week to catch rainwater, and the role the sun and moon play in amplifying

---

21. "Water Facts," US Bureau of Reclamation.

your intentions and magical practices through tea witchery. You will also learn how to charge water with natural water sources as well as with the cycles of the moon from a bottle, tap, or purifier.

My intention with this chapter is that when you have finished reading it, you not only come away with a deeper appreciation for water but are also inspired to try new ways of tapping into the magnitude of water's seemingly endless magic, power, and benefits with all things tea witchery.

Disclaimer

The information in this chapter is for educational purposes only. If you are interested in accessing water in nature, please consult with your local authorities to make sure the water source you are using is healthy to drink. Unfortunately, in many regions of the world, natural unfiltered water is not safe to consume.

It is not responsible to use water from lakes, rivers, streams, or even rainwater for tea. Sewage, fertilizer, and many known and unknown bacteria and harmful elements are in the water that can cause serious health issues. Therefore, it is advisable to use a proper filtration system to drink water. It is also worth noting that some water is so alkaline (meaning it has a pH of seven or higher) it is not safe to drink even with a filtration system. Although it is acceptable to use water from natural sources in ceremonial rituals, it is not recommended to drink it.

Just because it is not safe to drink water from some natural water sources does not mean these sources are not a powerful aid for magical workings, meditation, scrying, or stone cleansing. With that in mind, to get the most out of this chapter, and harness the natural power of water, it is recommended that you place your clean, filtered water into a secure container and bring this to natural water sources. Doing this will allow your water to be charged by the energy and power of your chosen water source. I will share with you how to do this later in the chapter, in the section called Charging Your Water with Natural Water Sources on page 55.

Water Is Living

When brewing a magical cup of tea, there are plenty of layers and elements to consider. The first, if not the most important, is the water you choose. Clean, pure water is the best to enhance and bring out the subtleties of the tea's flavors and color.

It has been said that water is living and that it has its own consciousness. It is important for each of us to remember, as much as humans and earth are made up of water, there is only so much water on the planet. Therefore, our love and respect of water should not go unnoticed, as our energy, thoughts, and feelings are imprinted on to water. This has been proven in a variety of studies, most notably, through the work of Dr. Masaru Emoto, who showed that the molecular structure of water can be altered through human consciousness.[22]

What does this all have to do with tea and the fact that water remembers it is living? Water is naturally recycled, and in this process, water remembers its various living experiences.

Water, as ice melts, is then evaporated into the sky to form clouds, and then rained back down to the earth. Water from all other sources—oceans, rivers, lakes—is also caught in this osmosis pattern of ascension to be released and redispersed as rain. Therefore, not only does water have many lives, and thus countless ways in which it interacts with earth and all of life, but it can remember these experiences. This accumulative set of experiences plays a role in how it affects all life on this planet, including how it is used in tea.

Water is the life force of the planet—bleeding, healing, flowing, rushing, calming, renewing. All of this is done throughout every second of every day. Water directly from the earth or off the earth is both earth power and water power. You get the benefits of working with water that has been supercharged with the power and strength of earth. When you are brewing a magic cup of tea or herbal potion, I invite you to consciously consider your sources for water and its representation in your magical tea, tisane, potion, or liquid spell craft.

The next section of the chapter will detail eight different ways to access fresh water from nature and the metaphysical and health correspondences of these different sources of water, especially when brewed with your tea.

---

22. Emoto, *The Hidden Messages in Water.*

Fresh Water Sources

If you are lucky enough to have access to nature's finest and purest of waters and springs, you are blessed. When using water direct from nature, there should be a few guidelines. The first thing to consider is the source. Is it pure enough to directly drink from? This is especially important when considering natural pools, streams, rivers, lakes, waterfalls, or rain and storms.

Unfortunately, due to a variety of issues, many of our world's fresh water sources have been tainted. This makes it quite dangerous to take in the water without a proper filtration system along with a clear understanding of the elements in the water.

Despite the tainted water sources, there are still many opportunities to experience these fresh water sources and harness their power if you seek them out. If you are concerned about the cleanliness of the water, even in nature, do not fret. As referenced in the disclaimer at the beginning of this chapter, you can place your clean, filtered water into a secure container and bring this to natural water sources to be charged.

Another way of purifying water from natural sources is bringing the water to a boil before brewing your tea with it. This eliminates any bacteria that may be harmful to you. You are also using the heat source as a representation of the element of fire to ignite and give energy to your will and intention of the water and its purpose in your tea.

Headwaters

The term *headwaters* refers to water that comes directly from the earth. In most cases, it is pure and will make the best cup of tea for meditation. This type of fresh source water will clear the mind and balance your body, aligning you closer to Mother Earth and your true intentions of being.

Headwaters are said to fuel your soul and heal what may be ailing you. Consider your tea, herbs, and intentions when enjoying this sacred cup brewed directly from the source of the spring or river.

River Water

River water is an excellent choice when the goal of your inner work, meditation, or potion is to move on and clear a new path. River water is helpful when focusing on new goals, as it can aid in the drive and desire to accelerate your intended success. River water also opens the mind for new ideas and helps release creativity.

Whether your intent is focused on an idea, plan, project, clearing obstacles, or cleansing illness, river water brewed with an energizing tea or herb combination will help bring swiftness and dedication to your intent.

Stream Water

Stream water has more of a slow-and-steady-wins-the-race vibration. Stream waters are persistent and delicate; therefore, stream water in your tea is ideal for creating harmony, guidance, and nourishment, releasing negativity, and facilitating growth and abundance.

Stream water also slows down manic thoughts to allow focused thinking to occur. A cup of tea and herbs charged with or brewed with this water helps to organize thoughts and project ideas. Stream water can also be a harmonious cup while organizing the home and clearing away small clutter and small annoyances that may be clogging your thoughts.

Lake Water

Lake water is still and calm, making it ideal for deep thinking, reflection, memory recall, and access to what the water remembers. Because of this, lake water is a great source of bringing you closer to the Akashic Records, which recalls information and answers once considered lost.

Lake water also helps to instill peace and contentment. When lake water is used to brew or charge tea, it can bring a quality of fulfillment and happiness to your gathering, friends, and family. It can help cool hot tempers and short fuses, and aid in calming arguments and disagreements, be it in business or personal relationships.

Waterfall Water

Waterfall water is used to create power and energy. Waterfall water symbolizes success and the inner power to make things happen. With the added force of nature to open new doorways, waterfall water overflows with abundance and successes into your teacup.

Use this water to charge or brew a tea consumed at a celebration. This water is invigorating and adds a level of unstoppable confidence and drive to projects, speeches, and business. Waterfall water also adds an extra element of refreshment to iced tea.

Well Water

Well water has a long history of wish magic. It brings with it a deep insight, which is ideal for strengthening intuition and calling forth wishes into physical reality. Water remembers, and when you imbue well water that has been wished upon, you are acting as a facilitator of wish fulfilment and manifestation of hopes, dreams, and desires.

Charging your purified and filtered water next to or in well water fills your heart and mind with endless hope, desire, ambition, and aspirations. Well water tea also calls forth the energy of wellness and well-being because you are drinking water directly from the earth. Therefore, this water aids in facilitating an energized healing quality as you take in the water and its hydrating, cell-renewing benefits.

Snow Water

Charging your water with melted snow for tea is all about transformation and positive change. Use melted snow when you are transforming into a new person or position, or elevating your divination and Divine witchery.

Snow water tea will help solidify creative ideas and assist with successful business contracts. Melted snow in tea can be symbolic of melting away a hard exterior, both in yourself and someone else, helping to improve relationships of all kinds.

If you make tea using snow, then refreeze the tea into ice cubes to be added to iced tea and served during business meetings or creative gatherings. This will help solidify the intention of the gathering and manifest those ideas into physical reality. This method will also work to bring families into a tighter bond.

Rainwater

Rainwater has an abundance of uses and is multifaceted with layers of influences. In general, rainwater is used to promote growth, change, cleansing, emotional balance, and physical well-being.

The best way to collect rainwater for tea drinking is to use a large silver metal soup pot or large open-mouth glass or ceramic bowl. The intent is to collect as much rainwater as you need for conjuring tea magic. You can collect extra rainwater for later use if you like, but if you pour it into jars and save for later, do not forget to date and title them. I would also invite you to write loving intentions and even metaphysical symbols on the jars to amplify the intentions and energy in the water.

If you are saving rainwater for later or using it right away, be sure to bring the rainwater to a boil before drinking it. Remember, by bringing it to a boil this will remove toxins to purify and ready the tea and rainwater magic to be taken internally. The fire source will activate intentions as it boils the water to purify it. This is symbolic of removing doubts and easing the mind, which is a perfect place of inner peace to be in to fully enjoy a cup of tea.

If you are concerned about the purity of rainwater in your region, you can place a closed water jug that contain your purified filtered water outside. The rainwater will help charge your water and the effects of this will still be highly beneficial.

Power of Rainwater and Rain's Correspondence

The power of rainwater comes from the sky, the Divine, and the great unknown. Rain is water magic whipped with air, wind, sometimes electrified with lightning, and then soothed by soft rays of sun. To catch rainwater to make tea with is to collect water that holds the charge of all the elements, and sometimes the magical power of rainbows.

Although it is ideal to catch enough rainwater to brew an entire cup or pot of tea, if you are only able to catch a little bit of rain, that small bit is still useful. You can add it to a kettle of water that you plan to make tea with. The intent here, and the correspondence, is imprinted into the amount you caught. You may want to keep some of this water in your curio, taking out just a teaspoon or so and adding it to your cup or pot as needed for meditation, tea rituals, and potion work.

As you can see, rainwater is both powerful and, depending on where you reside, plentiful. It offers many healthy and potently magical uses with tea. You may think there is only one kind of rainwater but there are actually thirteen different variations of rainwater, with dozens of different correspondences. In this section I will share insights on all thirteen.

Spring Rain

Spring rain can be used to brew up passion and excitement. Examples can range from new relationships and romantic partners to business deals. Spring rain is excellent for planting ideas and seeds, and manifesting new adventures.

Using spring water is ideal when you are brewing a tea to attract a lover or new friends. Spring rain is charged with new growth and carries a vibration of new beginnings, love, breakthroughs, and excitement.

Summer Rain

Summer rain is refreshing and deeply relaxing. Collecting this type of rain can lend to personal growth and boosting creative ideas. This type of rain can keep abundance flowing and keep your heart and mind happy.

Summer rainwater tea helps to lift depression by adding the energy of the sun to a gloomy feeling. Summer rainwaters also make thirst-quenching iced teas.

Fall Rain

Fall rain is crisp and invigorating, bringing deep gratitude to your cup of tea and warmth to your heart. Fall is a time for giving thanks and for sharing abundance, which makes fall rain ideal for brewing a pot of tea to share the intent of gratitude and abundance with family, friends, business associates, deities, and ancestors.

Gratitude and abundance are not just for the fall season. It is recommended to be thankful year-round for your blessings. This includes the people in your life, the things you have, lessons you have learned, and the experiences that have played a role in setting you free. That being said, when you use the energy of fall rain in your tea, and weave this into your gratitude and abundance rituals, you are amplifying two of the most powerful set of intentions with one of the best types of rainwater for this type of tea witchery.

Winter Rain

Winter rain is fantastic for calling forth stability and strength of foundations. Winter is a time when we reflect on all that has come and gone. Winter rainwater makes the inside warmer, whether it is your home, body, or spirit.

A cup of cold winter rainwater brewed into tea will lend you strength to move forward to brighter days as you release all that is no longer necessary for your journey. Winter rainwater will help ease away negativity from your past and prepare you for new beginnings, sustaining your well-being into the season of spring and beyond. Choose your tea and herbs to lend extra inspiration and warmth to this brew of tea or potion.

Deep Heavy Rain

Deep heavy rain is life-giving and thought-provoking. This makes this kind of rainwater useful for tea magic when you want to help wash away negativity and cleanse emotional blockages. Because of this, deep heavy rainwater aids in forgiveness and apologies.

Deep heavy rain is a powerfully healing rainwater that is charged and ready to help ease troubled times. It will help facilitate change by softening the earth and, metaphorically, softening difficult situations and troubles.

Lightning Storm Rain

Lightning storm rain is electrifying and powerful. This kind of rainwater is collected for tea during a lightning storm. It brings enhanced empowerment to all magical brews, magical workings, and powerful tea-leaf readings.

Lightning storm water can be used to bring new energy and revitalized thinking when meditating with tea. This water also brings information lightning fast and supercharged.

A word of caution: when collecting lightning storm rain you should not stand outside due to the risk of being struck by lightning. As previously suggested, there are many ways for collecting rainwater safely that do not place you in any danger.

Place a large soup pot, large open-mouth glass jar, or ceramic bowl outside and then collect your rainwater after the lightning passes.

Sun and Rain

When it is raining and the sun is shining, this type of rainwater is infused with fire and is very powerfully charged for happiness, growth, balance, and prosperity. This is great water to add to your tea to help bring balance to a relationship or balance to your body.

Sun and rain also make for perfect water to use if you are balancing gender neutrality in your body or becoming harmonious with duality. A cup of tea made with this water will give you energy, aid in lifting depression, and help to balance manic thoughts. This is incredibly helpful and healing water that can also bring unexpected abundance, especially if you see the rainbow with it.

Rainbow Rain

Rainbow rain just may be the luckiest of all rains to make tea with. Charged with the sun and infused with the energies of hope and luck, using the pot of gold at the end of the rainbow theory, a cup of tea with this magically charged water can bring luck, unexpected abundances, and golden opportunities.

Rainbow water imprints the seven colors of the rainbow on to the water as it falls from the sky into your collection basin. Color therapy itself is a powerful healing aid. I invite you to explore the deeper psychological, emotional, and meta-physical correspondences of the primary colors permeating the rainbow.

There is, however, another color that plays a role in the potency of rainbow rain, but it is not necessarily a color that shows up. This is gold. There are the golden rays of the sun, but there are also additional ways that gold is infused into rainbow rain.

Rainbow energy is heavily steeped in ancient folklore and legend, most notably Celtic folklore that says at the end of every rainbow is a pot of gold. Therefore, you can call on these energies and correspondences of gold to be infused into your tea. Examples of golden ideas, golden prosperity, golden wisdom, and sometimes the golden rule are additional energies and intentions that help make rainbow rain especially potent when you are adding this to your tea and potion brewing.

It is also important to remember the seven colors of the rainbow align themselves with the seven colors of the chakra points in our bodies and our aura field. I also invite you to take some time to learn more about the chakras, as they are the energy centers of our body.

Rainbow tea water, therefore, allows you to imbue, recharge, strengthen, and harmoniously balance your chakra system, which helps to aid in healing your body, mind, and spirit. This releases unwanted, negative, or emotional blocks that you may have, making rainbow rainwater a wonderful source for strengthening your life force energy.

Rainbow rain is helpful to place your healing intent into this cup by clearly visualizing the rainbow beaming down and swirling in your cup. As you drink in the essence, imagine these powerful colors and the vibration they carry entering your body through your mouth and filling your head with their graces. Feel into its energy as it moves down through your body and out of the soles of your feet, leaving you feeling completely energized and whole.

Wind and Rain
Wind and rain are stormy and can be collected or used to charge your water to aid in breakthroughs, with an intent to remove obstacles, both seen and unseen. Wind and rainwater also help you release negative feelings, making it easier to release beliefs, behaviors, and relationships that no longer serve you.

Wind and Rainstorm with Lightning
This type of rainwater is commonly found in tornados, hurricanes, and violent weather patterns, which does not necessarily lend itself to easy collecting. When you can safely capture this type of storm water, it will help to remove curses, hexes, and dark energies that you feel you might have attached to you.

A strong cup of tea charged with this water facilitates banishment and removal of harmful energy. Bathing in this water or standing in this type of storm (only when and where it can safely be done) cleanses unwanted energies, entities, and bad vibrations that may have attached to you.

Full Moon Rainwater

Full moon rainwater is not easy to catch, but when you do this, it helps to create a most delightful cup of tea for heightening intuition in your tea leaf readings. Since the rainwater is directly touched by the light of the silver moon herself, this water is charged with the Divine feminine and lends itself perfectly as an offering to goddesses or other female deities you might be working with.

Full moon tea water can enhance intuition and psychic abilities. It is worth noting, however, that full moon rainwater tea can be a little unpredictable—in a good way. What I mean is that it can bring a charge of uncontrollable laughter to your heart and lips. It can also inspire you to dance, sing, and make magical things.

Full moon water can be collected in the day too, although it may be a little weaker in its charge. If it is raining during the day of a full moon, be sure to grab some. You can always leave it out later that night under the potency of the full moon or in a window where the moonlight can reach it to recharge.

Blue Moon Rainwater

Blue moon rainwater is exceedingly rare and probably the hardest to plan for. This rainwater in magical tea supersedes full moon properties and powers, adding an element of miracles. Use this water for tea meditation when you are divining deep inward for answers and are open and ready to accept and receive a miracle.

New Moon Rainwater

New moon rainwater occurs during the time in which the moon is dark, or at its smallest crescent. This type of rainwater makes a tea that will inspire you to look deep inside yourself to find and fix the things that have been bothering you or causing you problems. This new moon charged tea is for deep personal meditation and tea magic.

When working with new moon rainwater, be open to seeing, acknowledging, and correcting wrongs you may have made. Be open to forgiving those who have wronged you as you sip this super-charged tea. You can also serve tea charged by new moon rainwater to others who might need a little help seeing inside themselves.

Water and the Days of the Week

Another layer to add to rainwater tea witchery are the days of the week you catch the rain. Yes, the days of the week absolutely play a role in the potency of the rain and their correspondences. Combining your magical tea and rainwater work with the days of the week aids in empowering your intentions, which helps to accelerate your desires coming to fruition.

Monday

Monday is ruled by the moon and is aligned with feminine energy. Monday represents women's wisdom, mysteries, beauty, fertility, and emotions as the moon rules the waters' tides.

Monday is the best day to work water magic, tea leaf reading, tea and water scrying, and tea magic. Monday is the day the earth plane is closest to the astral plane, making this is an auspicious day for your tea witchery to enhance astral projection, dream magic, tea and water scrying, and deep meditation.

Teas and herbs that resonate with Monday include jasmine tea, oolong tea, lemon balm, raspberry leaf, catmint, lemon peel, white willow bark, rose hips, and jasmine flowers.

Tuesday

Tuesday is ruled by Mars and is aligned with masculine energy. Powerful intentions to make on Tuesday include ambition, competition, lust, reversal of hexes, and repelling psychic attacks. This is a good day to drink tea that builds strength mentally and spiritually. It is also an ideal day to amplify protection work.

Teas and herbs that resonate with Tuesday include white tea, lapsang souchong tea, basil, ginger, blessed thistle, and ginseng.

Wednesday

Wednesday is ruled by Mercury and is aligned with masculine energy. Powerful intentions to make on Wednesday include communication, mental clarity, transportation, luck, and chance. This is a good day to drink teas associated with prosperity, luck, and good business. Mercury is the bringer of quick cash, making this an auspicious day to brew a money and successful business tea.

Teas and herbs that resonate with Wednesday include green tea, lavender, mint, caraway, fennel seed, licorice root, orange peel, and cinnamon.

Thursday

Thursday is ruled by Jupiter and is aligned with masculine energy. Thursday brings abundance, prosperity, wealth, protection, and personal strength, and serves as a facilitator of masculine fertility. Thursday is a good day to sign contracts and acquire assets. It is an excellent day to brew a tea to aid in visualization and meditation of future successes and long-term wealth. Thursday is also the best day to brew up tea and magic to aid in justice or court cases.

Teas and herbs that resonate with Thursday include dragonwell green tea, clove, star anise, dandelion leaf, ginseng, nutmeg, horny goat weed, goldenseal, lemon peel, and calendula.

Friday

Friday is ruled by Venus and is aligned with feminine energy. Friday is a wonderful day for love, pleasure, romance, marriage, attractions, friendships, and affairs of the heart. Friday is the traditional day for all things love related. This is also a perfect day for blending and sharing love teas and healing-heart teas.

Teas and herbs that resonate with Friday include black tea, oolong, rose, cardamom, thyme, vanilla, passionflower, ginger, pomegranate, damiana, hibiscus, and red clover.

Saturday

Saturday is ruled by Saturn and is aligned with feminine energy. Intentions that are ideal for this day include wisdom, banishing, cleansing, and protection. Saturday is the best day to focus on releasing what no longer serves you, banishing unwanted energies, and binding that which has done you wrong. This means banishing sickness and aiding in help to end a disease. This is a great day to drink tea associated with clear thinking, health, and power enhancement.

Saturday is also the preferred day to work with the dead and communicate with ancestors who have crossed over. Sharing a cup of tea with your ancestor can facilitate communication and guidance, providing answers you may be seeking. Folklore says Saturday is the best day for locating lost items or missing people.

Teas and herbs that resonate with Saturday include Assam black tea, cinnamon, St. John's wort, licorice root, sunflower petals, clove, and valerian root.

Sunday

Sunday is ruled by the sun and is aligned with masculine energy. The sun is the largest celestial body in our solar system. It is on fire, giving life and shining bright. Sunday is the perfect day to engage in big stuff, to activate and give spark to desires and goals, activating change, wealth, hope, vitality, joy, and healing.

The intent that Sunday brings is power, happiness, success, fame, and promotions. This is also a day of bright beginnings, making it a wonderful opportunity to drink in all that life has to offer and activate yourself with a tea that brings you happiness and joy.

Teas and herbs that resonate with Sunday include black tea, rooibos, orange pekoe, orange peel, chamomile, ginseng, bay leaves, calendula, and sunflower petals.

Charging Your Water with Natural Water Sources

If you cannot catch enough water from the sky or you do not feel safe drinking water from natural water sources, there are alternative methods to harnessing this energy into your water to be used for tea. Charged water for tea, whether it is from a bottle, the tap, or a purifying system, can all be charged with added enhancements and attributes of the elements, the four directions, and the moon and by nature's own sources of water. Later in the book, in the chapter on tea rituals and moon magic, I share a process for charging water with the moon cycles. For this section, we will begin with a focus on charging your water via the ocean.

Charging with Ocean Water

The oceans contain an undeniable amount of power and energy. That is why the ocean is synonymous with cleansing, healing, and banishing or letting go. The ocean also symbolizes fertility and life force. Ocean water is not for drinking and should never be consumed with your tea or anything you drink. It can be, however, a powerful source for your magical workings.

You may use ocean water to cleanse your tea tools, such as your favorite tea-pot, teacups, or tea infusers to rid them of magical residue or past workings. But again, ocean water is not for teamaking to drink or ingestible potion making.

You can charge your drinking water with ocean water. This can be done by putting your drinking water in a jug right down into the ocean water with you. Using your manners of please and thank you, ask the ocean to charge this water for your tea and magical potions with its healing energy and renewal of life. You may also ask the ocean to lend its power to release unwanted attachments, negativity, beliefs, values, or behaviors that no longer serve you. The ocean can charge your water with abundance, strong life force or chi, and the blessings of fertility and growth.

Another way to harness the vibration and frequency of the ocean is to bring your jug of water to the beach and settle it on the sand where you will be sitting. Speak your intentions and allow it to soak in the rays of the sun, the misty breeze, the warmth of the sand, and the sounds of the crashing waves. This water will carry the beach vibration and frequency.

When taking this water that has been charged by the ocean to make your tea, you can choose to make a hot cup of tea on that same day to bring back the meditative and calming elements of the ocean. You could also put it in your teapot and savor it on a day that a little ocean vibration is needed.

Water charged with the ocean's potent power also makes great ice cubes for other drinks, adding its cooling and refreshing ocean vibration to anything you are drinking. Or go an extra step and use it to make iced tea or sun tea for an extra boost of summertime fun.

Charging Water at High Noon

Charging your water in the high noon sun will add the full power of the sun's fiery passion, drive, ambition, and strength to your tea and drinkable potion waters. With the sun in the highest place of the day, this energy is at the pinnacle for sun energy infusion.

High noon sun also carries the energetic balance of day and night, drawing up to its highest point to now turn quietly into the darker hours. This water is good for balancing arguments, allowing each of the opponents to see the other side of the issue.

Using high noon water for your tea not only lends you the aspects of drive, ambition, and fiery passion, but it also helps you to balance excitement and creates an easy transition to fruition and completion.

Sun Tea

Whether it be a tea with fiery drive and balanced intentions, or an amazing full-flavored tea brewed in the sun with the intent of quenching your thirst, high noon water makes the best sun tea. This is because you are infusing your tea and herbs directly under the flames of the sun, energizing and igniting all your intentions that are woven into your jar.

The absolute best thing for making sun tea is a glass jug. There are many on the market; lots of them already come with a spigot on the bottom of the jar for easy dispensing. You can also reuse and repurpose a large glass gallon jar.

Black tea bags make the best and most classic sun and iced tea. Depending on your flavor pallet and how strong you like your tea will determine how many tea bags to use.

Here is a basic guideline for making the most powerful and tasty sun tea:

+ Use eight standard-size tea bags for a gallon of sun tea.
+ Place tea bags into a gallon jar that is filled with clean filtered water. If you like weaker tea, you can experiment with using two or three tea bags. The opposite applies if you like stronger tea, as you can experiment using nine or ten tea bags.
+ Place and tighten the lid on the jar and set in the sun for three to four hours.
+ If you like your tea sweet, add your sweeteners before placing into the sun. Doing so will give the sun the opportunity to slowly melt and dissolve the sugar into the water.
+ If you are a honey or agave person, you can add these types of liquid sweeteners when tea is finished. They easily dissolve into the tea without needing to be warmed first like sugar.

+ If you are working with infusing balance into your sun tea, be sure to place the tea in the sun between 10:00 a.m. and 2:00 p.m. Doing this will give the tea the energy and intent of two hours before high noon and then amplifying the charge of high noon with a balance of the two hours after high noon.

+ When your desired flavor is perfected, remove the tea bags from the jar. The tea is absolutely the best for enjoying right at this point.

+ Fill a glass with ice cubes and pour your sun tea over the ice. Enjoy!

If you wish you can transfer the tea out of the glass jar and into a more refrigerator-friendly container or a pitcher that is easier to pour from. Sun tea will keep in the refrigerator with a lid or cover over the top for up to three to four days.

Full Moon and Sun Energy

If you are seeking to establish a supremely balanced sun tea, try charging your water by the light of the full moon, followed by making sun tea the next day. This tea will hold the balanced charge of both the sun and the moon, which harnesses the energy of fire and ice.

The moon, sun, fire, and ice are all powerful sources of energy. For this reason, choose your teas and herbs wisely when you enact this tea preparation ritual. Use proper correspondences and be clear with your intent and intended outcome for this tea or tisane.

This strongly charged tea will bring enhanced balanced thinking to your meditations, helping you to become more productive with better follow-through and will help to bring enemies to an agreeable reconciliation.

Fusing together these four powerful energies can be a magical tea preparation ritual that will aid in the connecting and balancing of gender neutrality issues, bringing forth a smooth transition and balanced control. Thus, full moon plus sun energy equals mental, emotional, spiritual, and sexual harmony.

Next Steps with the Vital Liquid

As you have learned, water is many things. Above all, it is the vital liquid of life itself. Water is also a connection and a metaphor that links us to the flow of the collective unconsciousness, which many refer to as the Akashic Records. The Akashic Records are where one can reach in, access Divine sight, and seek out answers from all directions of time in the universe. It is well known that in ancient times, witches, wisdom keepers, and shamans would sit by a calm body of water and watch its flowing motion create patterns so that they would then interpret, bringing forth insights and answers from the Akashic Records.

This form of hydromancy is not only still used today but it has matured into what is known as teacup scrying, which the next chapter is devoted to.

Whether it was at a large water source or in the small space of a teacup, sometimes a spirit would appear in the water and bring a telepathic message. Water spirits and sea creatures were often first seen in water meditation, scrying, and hydromancy and then shared with the family or village in stories. Often these insights were interpreted as messages from the gods and Akashic Records and leaned into as predictions of the future.

Hydromancy and teacup scrying are not just ancient methods of divination through water; they are modern-day art form, especially with tea witchery. Both hydromancy and teacup scrying involve time and focus to hone your abilities to initiate focus from inside the mind so that the visions will then create themselves on the surface of the water. With that in mind, learning the art form of teacup scrying is the next step on your journey to mastering tea witchery.

Chapter 5

The Art of Teacup Scrying

Tea is a meditative and intimate activity that can gently carry you away into deep thought and self-hypnosis before you even realize you are going on a magical mystery tour. When drinking tea, it is not uncommon for visions to spontaneously occur. Tea is water, accented with earth in the form of tea, flowers, herbs, and spice. As you have learned in the previous chapter, water is not only an element that is sacred and incredibly powerful but it's also the essential foundation for tea. Therefore, when we ingest or imbue tea, water is carried to each cell of our being, nourishing us, and connecting us to the ever-flowing river of life. However, that is not all tea connects us to.

Tea is a warm sensation where the inhalation of scent from the steam activates the olfactory senses and carries the vapors of water and tea into the deepest recesses of memory. In this capacity, tea can act as an inner guide to unlocking the mysteries of the individual consciousness and collective conciseness. Tea is a multidimensional key to accessing the Akashic Records when paired up with proper intention, focus, and meditation. For all these reasons, and more, tea is a perfect conduit for hydromancy.

Hydromancy (from Greek words *hydro* and *manteia*, meaning *water* and *divination*, respectively) is the art of gazing by means of water. This includes divination using physical characterisitics of water such as the color, ebb and flow, or ripples produced by pebbles tossed or the movement of air. Water scrying, also known as hydromancy, is the most ancient of all divining sight methods. In this chapter, you are going to learn about the art form of teacup scrying.

Nostradamus the Water Gazer

The first scrying on water is said to go back to times of the old paths and legends, of myths and gods, when answers would be drawn from the reflection of a still lake when the moon was full or waxing. Perhaps the most famous of all water gazers is Michel de Nostredame, better known as Nostradamus.

Living between the years of 1503 and 1566, Nostradamus was a French astrologer, physician, and renaissance seer. In modern times, he is known more for his eminence and controversial history of predicting future events. I wonder if he knew he would occupy a small section of a chapter on teacup scrying.

Nostradamus's book of 942 poetic quatrains published in 1555, which allegedly predicted future events and prophesies, has rarely been out of print since his death in 1566.[23] Some of his predictions, prophesies, and visions are still agonized and scrutinized over to this day, nearly five hundred years later, as evidenced in the number of books, articles, and references in documentaries that cite his achievements. While I am not going to delve into his predictions, I do want to share with you Nostradamus's method of water scrying. Rarely do you hear about his magical workings with water when his name comes up, either in personal conversations or mainstream references of Nostradamus.

For all that has been written about Nostradamus, including his own writings, there is little known about his method of predictions. This is how he wanted it, for he did not detail much about his process when he was alive. What is known is that he used a brass bowl of water placed on a tripod, and added vibration and sound by tapping the bowl with a wand or stick. He would sometimes add aromatic herbs to the water.

While in a trance-like, hypnotic state, Nostradamus would gaze for hours into the water and the patterns that materialized from his tapping on the bowl. It was

---

23. "Five Facts of Nostradamus That You Probably Didn't Know and Ten Events About the World He Knew All Too Well," India Today.

also written that the room in which he would gaze was dimly lit. The reason for this is that less light gave clarity for the mind's eye to singularly focus on the water and the ripples in the water.

What I find most fascinating is that Nostradamus found his method for reaching information within the scented flow of water, the stillness of water, and in the vibrational ripples of water. Although we may never know the precise nature of how he engaged in water scrying, I can confidently say that there is a direct and replicable process that you can apply in your teacup scrying that Nostradamus and many other alchemists, sages, witches, oracles, and those curious about magic have engaged in for centuries.

How Teacup Scrying Works

Teacup scrying works in similar ways to hydromancy and water scrying, only the vessel is a teacup and the medium is tea. Like all practices of tea witchery, choose your tools and prepare them with conscious thought, joy, and consecration.

Your teacup should have no designs on the inside of the cup. This is to avoid interfering with the tea and water patterns. Choosing your tea is an important part of the process. Later in this chapter, I explain how different teas can help you reach your objective with teacup scrying. This involves using the properties of the tea plant or the aid of herbs and flowers to lend their abilities and vibrations to your brew, delivering clearer and more specific visions.

Here is a simple process to follow with teacup scrying. I refer to this as syncing yourself with the energy of the tea:

- When your tea is brewed, place the teacup on the table and sit down in the chair in front of it. If you can do this outside under a full moon, even better.
- Take at least three measured breaths, slowly exhaling, so that you can ease into a relaxed state. When you are ready, gaze into your teacup.
- Allow your vision to blur and your mind to relax.
- Hold your concentration, keep your focus, and breathe in the essence of the tea.

+ You may find it helpful to rock gently back and forth or in a slow steady circular motion while you gaze. This will further assist you to align your body with the slow vibrations of the tea water, allowing you to pick up on messages easier.
+ Your sight should begin to blur like water. Hold still, try not to blink, and hold your concentration on the blurriness for as long as you can.

Water is always moving and vibrating even when it appears still. It is these micro movements that help to lull your mind into a soft, trance-like state. Your mind's eye will begin to sync up with the vibration and movement of the water.

If you are new to teacup scrying or water gazing, you may want to mindfully spend time working on holding your concentration and focus on water, especially around not blinking for as long as is comfortable for you. Remember, teacup scrying, like all forms of hydromancy, is an art form and requires dedication, respect, and practice.

If your eyes begin to water from not blinking and holding the gaze, allow these tears to flow as an offering of water to water. These tears often aid in the blur of the trance and vision. Feel your head grow light then heavy, observe the sensations in your body, and relax into them. When you step outside of your eyes and slip into a trance-like state, this is where you immerse yourself into what the water and tea is sharing with you.

The Gatekeepers

When practicing teacup scrying, be ready for the gatekeepers. When looking deep within the realms of otherworldly seeing, sometimes the first images that comes to mind or dance on the water are of a darker nature. For instance, sometimes strange scenes, faces, and feelings can arise. Acknowledge what is showing up without breaking concentration and then simply move past them. Do not be frightened by what shows up as they have no power over you or your visions. They are simply the gatekeepers of information.

The more you practice teacup scrying, the more at ease you will become and the deeper your understanding of the experience will be. Also, the more well versed you are in the art form of teacup scrying, the easier the syncing up of your mind's eye with the vibration of the tea and water will become.

Some people report when scrying that they slip right into a clear trance of lucid vision and vibration within a few minutes of dedicated focus. They can watch images unfold and interpret messages and symbols with ease. If this has happened for you, that is wonderful. If you are new to teacup scrying or you have dabbled in it but have not derived any visions, do not worry. The more you open yourself to the process, the more fun it will be and the more adept you will become in the art form of teacup scrying.

Choosing Your Tea and Herbs

In the process of teacup scrying, tea is your medium. Choosing the right tea or herb to scry or meditate with can enhance the frequency and vibration of your vision. For example, a cup of green tea can help energize and clear the mind, allowing you to quickly ease into meditation and receive insights.

Green tea was brought to Japan in the eighth century by a Buddhist monk named Dengyo Daishi who had been studying Buddhism in China. He had brought seeds to his monastery and planted them there. This elixir was so powerful and welcomed that the emperor of Japan was served tea at the monastery when he visited. The emperor was delighted by the tea and instructed tea to be planted and established in all five regions of Japan.[24]

When you choose green tea, be sure to add in a little dried ginkgo biloba leaf with your brew, as this will further assist in you remembering your thoughts and visions. This will also help you to hold your focus and meditative state longer.

Choosing a rich black tea, brewed dark and strong, can help you gaze deeper into layers of the abyss and seek your answers there. Like using a black mirror over a crystal ball, a dark tea provides a smooth surface to focus your gaze. This is a preference of color, sight, and focus, but the fundamental principles remain the same when you are seeking answers and insights via the surface of an object.

One of the best tea blends to prepare your mind for meditation and sight is one of the most popular Kitchen Witch Gourmet blends, which is called Clarity.

---

24. Pettigrew, *A Social History of Tea*.

Clarity

Here is the clear focus blend for Clarity, followed by a mantra I use with this tea.

- ½ cup of loose green tea such as dragonwell or sencha. This is to energize and awaken the mind.

- ¼ cup lemongrass. Lemongrass will help you center your mind, body, and breathing together.

- 2 tablespoons of dried ginkgo biloba. This will help you build memory, call into focus past lives and past lessons, and help reveal new lessons, which bring forth clearer answers.

- 1 tablespoon of lavender. Lavender will calm your mind to help you slip into a meditative state and relaxed body preparing you to receive information.

Once you have ingredients for Clarity, gather your herbs and tea, toss them together in a bowl, then place in a cool and dry container. Use Clarity by the cup or pot to gain clarity over situations, issues, and challenges you may encounter on your path. Clarity is useful for divinations. This tea blend also helps to unlock memories and forgotten moments.

I have developed a mantra that I like to chant while preparing to use Clarity for teacup scrying or other forms of hydromancy. It is based on the four elements:

Earth: Teacup of earth and sand, resting firmly in the palm of my hand.

Water: Purity of water, clear and deep. Clarity tea into the water steeps.

Fire: Stovetop with ease, I click to ignite. Bring what I seek into clear sight.

Air: The teacup I swirl—the water it twirls—the air releases fragrant pearls (of wisdom).

Conclusion: As the spirits that be, as above so below, allow me access to visions that flow.

Moonlight and Water Scrying

When you are preparing your teacup and teapots to be used in scrying, it is a good idea to treat all your tools with respect. This means preparing them for proper use that is aligned with the method of scrying and for the intentions you have set forth.

Since the moonlight and water scrying have been linked together from the beginning, it's only fitting that I use them as the basis for the following process.

Under the light of the full moon, or new moon, place your favorite teacups and teapot for scrying. Allow the moonlight to cover the cups and pot, bathing them in the glow of the moon for no less than one hour. If it is a new moon, you will likely not receive as much visible light as a full moon, but the energy and presence of the new moon is palpable. Fill a clear glass jar with water, enough to make a pot of tea. I always recommend preparing extra water under the moon to be used throughout the month. This is especially the case when there is added potency to specific moon cycles.

Charging Under the Full Moon

By absorbing the energy of the full moon into your water, cups, and pot, you have brought down the guiding light of the full moon to assist you in your quest for answers through scrying. The energy of the moon is now placed and set with intentions of clear sight into your tools and ready to assist you in your meditation. The light of the moon, now harnessed, will help illuminate answers, obstacles, and decisions that may present themselves in your scrying and meditation over the tea.

A full moon lasts approximately three days. You can charge your tools the entire three days if you choose. The minimum time for charging is at least one full hour.

You may also choose to place a clear quartz crystal into the water you are charging to amplify the water's clarity. That will in turn enhance the tea as a conduit for scrying.

Charging Under the New Moon

Absorbing the new moon energy into water and onto tea accessories can help you look deeper into hidden mysteries. The new moon's energy is used for looking for answers inside yourself. This moon helps to unlock and release issues you would like to change or remove. There is no light associated with the new moon; it is a time of darkness mostly credited with solemn and internal thoughts.

The new moons charge can help you see secrets and things that are hidden from view on mental, spiritual, and sometimes physical levels.

Just as you would do when charging under a full moon, you may also choose to place a clear quartz crystal into the water you are charging to amplify the water's clarity. That will in turn enhance the tea as an ideal conduit for scrying.

Scrying with Cream

A common accent to scrying in tea and coffee is the addition of milk or cream. The clouds that billow and swirl as they mix with the contents of the cup often have much to say. This form of divination happens quickly as the milk or cream will mix fluidly after the pour. These types of vision quests are mostly personal quick readings to do for yourself and not so much for others.

Here is a simple, four-step process for personal teacup magic. It is recommended to prepare your mind's eye right before the pour. Have one question to focus on and look for the symbols in the clouds. After the initial pour and burst of clouds, you can then slowly turn the cup to aid in the creation of vision. This folds the clouds, revealing new symbols, totems, and inspirations in the cup that can lead to a clearer interpretation of the answer you are seeking. Devour the vision and imbue the wisdom.

There is a notion that only milk should be added to black tea, that to add a heavier cream will distort the taste of the tea rendering it too milky. I am going to stand firm in my beliefs that if you like it a certain way then, by all means, enjoy it how you like it. As I say with all our tea blends, tea is "best brewed how the Kitchen Witch sees fit."

Taking this four-step process for personal teacup magic a step further, I have found that adding a pour of heavy whipping cream to your cup of black tea will create clouds and swirls that last much longer and are far more interesting and foretelling.

Heavy whipping cream works well because the heaviness of the fat and cream holds together longer in the cup, giving a deeper vision by creating richer layers in the cup. This works in all teas but works best in dark teas or coffee.

Tea Bags as Pendulums

I want to share with you a unique way to use prebagged tea in your teacup scrying practice by applying it as a pendulum.

Pendulums are a divination tool. A pendulum is a weight attached to a string or chain, allowing the weight to freely swing back and forth. Using a pendulum for divining answers is helpful when making decisions, especially when the question or decision can be summed up with a yes or no answer.

A pendulum raises the unconscious into the realm of your conscious awareness by bringing in the collective consciousness from the cosmos to guide you in a yes or no answer. To understand how this works is to understand that everything is energy. Everything around us vibrates at a specific level. As humans, we emit pulses of energy and vibration all the time. This is where that energy can be transferred into a pendulum.

By holding the pendulum steady in one hand, we allow our unconscious energy and vibration to run through our bodies down our arm into the pendulum. This unconscious vibration has now become conscious by delivering this energy to the pendulum, causing it to swing. The swing of a pendulum can take different directions. This includes back and forth, up and down, and round and round either to the left or right creating a circle.

If you have never worked with a pendulum for this type of divination, it is important to practice first with some simple questions. This way you are sure you understand how to receive answers and how the energy vibration works.

Here is a simple example to begin using your tea bag as a pendulum. First, speak an undeniable truth, such as your name. "My name is _____" (calmly state your name). The clear answer should be yes. Closely observe the movement of the tea bag as it moves in an up and down movement, like shaking your head yes. Now, speak a lie. "My name is _____" (except this time, say a different name). Watch as the pendulum slowly stops the yes movement and moves in a back and forth direction like shaking your head no.

When a pendulum moves in a circular motion, it is because of one or two things:

1. There is not enough information in the collective consciousness yet to guide this answer in a definitive direction.
2. There is too much conflicting energy in the room, which is blocking the correct answer from coming forth at that time.

Another way in which a pendulum works is that a clockwise direction is a yes and a counterclockwise circle is a no. It has been my personal experience that the faster the movement, the more solid the answer.

Now that you have the basics of how to work with a pendulum, I am excited to share with you some tips for how to transform your tea bag into a pendulum.

Holding your arm and hand steady, elbow off the table, lift the tea bag out of the tea. Hold it steady over the teacup. As the tea drips from the bag, think of your yes or no question with clear and centered focus, then ask your question. Allow the unconscious energy to flow through you and into your arm and then down into the tea bag. When dowsing with a tea bag as a pendulum, you get the added benefit of being able to also gaze into the teacup to scry and interpret any visions in the ripples that the tea bag has dripped into the tea.

Using a tea bag as a pendulum is a perfect accompaniment to any teacup meditation. Whether you are using an herbal tea or a classic tea, it can be done anytime and anywhere. A tea bag pendulum can be used when you are by yourself and need an answer for a question you are pondering. It is also a perfect divination tool when you are with a friend enjoying tea and your conversation may require an answer to a question.

This method can also be used if you use a tea ball to steep your tea with. This method of dowsing lets you customize your pendulum by choosing a tea or herbal blend that resonates with you and your higher self. You may also choose to create a blend that can help you scry deeper by unlocking deeper mysteries associated with a particular tea, herb, flower, or spice. This creates a potion that is aligned and charged with the essence of that plant and the magical or healing properties that are imprinted in it.

Next Steps with Teacup Scrying

I vividly remember my first encounter with teacup scrying, which happened during a tea leaf reading given to me many years ago at an enchanting metaphysical store in New Orleans. I intuitively knew this was a game changer for me. It was not as if I were asking myself consciously, "Okay, what are my next steps?" but I was invigorated to learn more about scrying and hydromancy, which would be infused into my unfolding journey in tea witchery.

I would never presume to know or assume how you are going to be called to journey into the art of teacup scrying, or other forms of water gazing. I would recommend, though, that if you are intrigued by the history of this ancient form of seeing into different realms and are seeking answers that have thus far eluded to, I invite you to revisit this chapter and allow your thirst for knowledge to guide you into your next steps.

For many of you who are being introduced to the divination tool of the pendulum for the first time, I encourage you to follow your curiosity and turn your bagged tea into a pendulum and ask some pressing questions you have been pondering. Of course, for those of you who are well steeped in the tradition of pendulums but perhaps have never considered the use of bagged tea as a divination tool, I invite you to give it a go next time you sit down with a cup of tea.

One final tip I would be remiss if I did not mention is to remember that your teaspoon is your magic wand. Consciously acknowledging this is important in your teacup scrying, as it adds potency and intention to the reading. This way, when you are looking for another way to facilitate movement in the water, tea, or clouds in the cream, you take your magic wand and tap the side of the cup with it. This allows the vibration to move the elements in your tea for you. This is a method that goes back for centuries in water gazing, when a brass bowl or glass bowl was used, such as the way Nostradamus would do.

Throughout the book I have mentioned the power of chants, incantations, and breath magic. In the next chapter, I am excited to share with you more details on how to make the most of your teacup scrying, and all things related to tea witchery through visualization, chants, incantations, and breath magic.

Chapter 6

Visualization, Chants, Incantations, and Breath Magic

A cup of tea is more than just magic; it is an intimate act. Intimacy is first set in motion with your choice of blends to match your desired mood and outcomes. This includes choosing a blend for specific healing needs, manifesting your desires, your momentary escapes, and satiating your lust for a flavor that delivers a satisfying conclusion to your chosen mood. Your environment, and how you are inspired to dress it up, also plays a role in the enhancement of overall intimacy and magical experience from enjoying your tea.

Beyond your choice of blends, there is something vitally important that comes first for creating intimacy and magic through tea. And that is visualization.

Before anything, you will want to visualize the experience you desire with your tea. Giving yourself the permission to feel into the intimate experience is an important element of tea witchery. In this chapter, I am going to share with you some effective and fun ways to visualize your inner desires for creating intimate, magical outcomes with your tea, but that is not all.

You are going to receive guidance on chants, incantations, and breath magic that you can apply to your own tea witchery. This includes how to call in gods and goddesses in your incantations as well as casting the I Love You tea spell.

To get started, we will begin where all magic does, from within.

Visualization

Visualizing your life's path and how you want to travel on it is a sacred art that requires dedication to your body, mind, and spirit. Creating all you want out of life through magical workings and tea witchery takes responsibility and care. You must make sure your visualizations are keeping in close alignment with the higher good of yourself and the space you carry around you, including the ones closest to you.

In whatever ways you choose to initiate your visualization, do your best to ensure it is a space where you can briefly close your eyes, and not be interrupted. Granted, that may not always be readily accessible. For instance, you may want to enjoy a cup of tea at work, where you are surrounded by coworkers. If you regularly drink tea at work, or you like to enjoy your tea in the company of others, your visualization process can be practiced beforehand, ensuring it is effective anywhere.

Whether it is done at home, in nature, in your office, or even in your car, the point is to set the intentions and visualization process in motion before you drink the tea. This can be done whether it is a few minutes before you prepare your tea or the night before. The more practice you have with visualizing, the more adept you will become at it, such as even doing this in a matter of seconds with your eyes open, while surrounded by people.

Four-Part Visualization Process

The following is a simple, four-part process for creating a magical life for yourself through visualizations. You can use this process as I have shared it here, but I also invite you to weave in your own distinct techniques and process to it. Above all, have fun.

Part 1

Creating a magical life for yourself through visualization begins by creating a truly clear vision of what it is you want. If it is more money you desire and you are wanting to engage in an abundance ceremony with your tea, give yourself the space to go beyond money as your primary desire. Rarely is a desire solely about money. Therefore, this is about feeling into what you believe the money can do for you. It is here you will get clear on the vision of what you want. Therefore, part one is allowing yourself to feel into your vision beyond the surface level desire.

Part 2

This is where you consciously reach inward with your sight, seeing and feeling into the energy and vibrations of your manifestations. You must see yourself doing or being what you desire and feeling what it would feel like. Inhale the emotion, knowing that in the space of feeling and seeing your desires, you are the thing you desire.

Part 3

Embody the quality of gratitude and appreciation for having, being, doing, and experiencing that which you desire. Allow yourself to feel deeply and genuinely grateful for this experience you desire, as if it has already happened, or is happening in that very moment. At some point, the voice of doubt may chime in and remind you that what you are offering gratitude for does not exist. Oh, but it does. Keep offering gratitude.

Part 4

The fourth part of visualization is trust and surrender, which are the essential ingredients that birth your dreams and desires into physical reality. Trust and surrender bridge the perceived gap between what you desire and the idea that it does not yet exist. Trust in the power of visualization and surrender, to the process of creation, knowing that what you desire exists in a specific vibration, in a specific dimension, both of which you are co-creating with the universe. Your desired manifestation exists and is waiting for you to vibrationally align with it. All you must do is rest in the comfort of trust, knowing that your magic is working.

Now What?

Once you have set the process in motion, give gratitude for the experience of visualization, and then go about your day. Or, if you are doing this immediately before your cup of tea, choose your blend and prepare your tea.

Whatever it is you are doing immediately following your visualization process, do not worry about when or how your desired outcome is going to manifest. Just know all the elements necessary for it to come into fruition are coming together on your behalf. Trust you have taken the required inner steps to embody your desire. The more aligned you are with your desire's vibration, the sooner you are reunited with your desire in a new, abundant reality.

Reconnect with Your Inner Sight

You may be familiar with visualization processes and techniques similar to the one you just read. If so, this four-part process might appear both simple and easy on the surface. Even so, if you have encountered challenges in the past with bringing your inner desires into an outer, physical reality, you are not alone in feeling that visualizing a magical life into your physical reality can feel quite daunting.

If you are anything like me and most of the world, we were raised and educated to only believe that which is real and true can be tangibly touched with our body and seen with our body's physical eyes. You know the old saying, "Seeing is believing"; well, that is true in its purest state. The way most people were taught to understand this, however, was from an inverted, outside-in perspective. This means people were unconsciously abandoning their inner sight by handing their trust for what is believed to be real over to the body's physical eyes.

"Seeing is believing," as most people know it, acts as a lower vibrational spell. It takes you away from your true inner sight, and does not serve anyone's highest good, including your workings with tea witchery. Therefore, to break free from whatever lingering hold this may have on you is to realign your trust from the inside-out. This means recalibrating your inner sight and placing your trust in that.

Your inner sight is one of your most powerful senses. This is how you see into the unknown. Reversing the inverted nature of "seeing is believing" silences self-doubt because you are now working from the inner realms with your magic.

Your inner sight is the eyes of your higher self. Your inner sight knows nothing of doubt, except that which your human self feeds into it, hence the reason it is called self-doubt. To reconnect with your inner sight, and build up trust with it, start by treating your inner sight like you would a newborn child. Give your inner sight unconditional love, nurturing its powers with delicate care, playing with it as you once played as a child, carefree where all things were possible. This is about giving your inner sight the mindful attention and intention necessary to mature and grow its power into its full, natural embodied essence.

Just know, any difficulties you have had with visualization before reading this book, they led you here. Be grateful for the contrast your past doubt taught you. Thank it for the lessons and then say goodbye to your past challenges.

As you practice the four-step visualization process, you are strengthening your inner sight, while simultaneously dissolving echoes of self-doubt. In fact, I invite you to engage in your own visualization practice with a farewell ceremony to self-doubt. Follow this up a celebratory tea ceremony welcoming in your newfound strength, trust, and gratitude for your inner sight.

Visualization Process with Your Tea

It is from your teacup cauldron you begin to visualize desired experiences and outcomes for intimacy and magical experiences with your tea. Here is a simple, yet powerful process for combining your tea with your visualization practice.

Choose the space you are going to visualize with your tea. Choose your desired blend of tea and prepare it. Bring forward into your mind's eye what it is you are seeking, creating, and manifesting.

The tea and water mix to form a potion to be taken internally, your intentions manifested outwardly. All the while you are consciously using your inner and outer being as the conductor of all things called forth from the quantum field of all possibility into your physical reality.

Now, visualize gently holding the cup of tea in the palms of your hands. See yourself slowly bringing it to your lips. The moment the steam rises, touching your skin, you feel it, inhaling the aroma of the tea blend. This intimate moment grows as the life force energy in the tea flows out of the cup and into your mouth, where you get your first taste of the flavor. This is the moment you ignite a spark of life in the power of your visualization when you are connected back to the vibration of your earlier visualization before drinking the tea.

It is in this magical moment you journey into the peaceful escape, where your chosen experience—be it your healing needs or the desires you seek—converge into this intimate act. You recognize and are grateful for the magic of it all, the wholeness of the experience held in a teacup, which is resting in the palms of your hands.

Breath Magic

Your breath holds the key to all that you do, as it carries your essence. This is air that has been taken inside of your very being, held close to your heart, and then released back out into the universe.

When you use your breath in a conscious manner and control what it is, you are imprinting your ideas and intentions onto your breath. Your breathing becomes a faithful friend, a trustworthy alliance on the multidimensional plane of manifestation and visualization. This is particularly true when working with tea witchery.

Air and water. Breath and tea. These are perfect tool combinations for manifesting and visualizing with tea. The sheer luxury of breathing, filling your lungs up with a deep inhalation of air and your surrounding space, only to exhale it back out into the universe, which then transforms it back into that vital life force commodity known as oxygen.

We all know that taking deep breaths can calm, center, and focus you. Conscious breathing, therefore, is an essential part of visualization. This is especially true when you are wanting to quiet the inner chatter to receive pristine clarity with your desires. To help you with your visualization and magical workings with tea witchery, you will want to catch your breath.

"Catching your breath" is a popular term that implies your need to slow down or rest. When someone wants to catch their breath, it is not uncommon to say out loud, "I'm out of breath," which is a foreboding thing to say out loud. This is because to say you are out of breath implies you are not breathing, which sends a distress signal to your body and mind you are dying. Certainly not the type of feeling or signal you want to be sending out when you are intending to enjoy an intimate and magical experience with your tea. So, take heed with the words and phrases you say, and do not use the term, "I'm out of breath."

Not only does your breath sustain your life force, but your breath also carries your words. Lending your words to your breath, the very essence of life force, imbues your words with life force power. Think of it this way: "words are magic, that's why it's called spelling."

When you take a deep conscious breath, allow it to fill your lungs and surround your heart, allowing your heartbeat to pulse its rhythm into the exhale. You just gave that breath the vital, life-sustaining force of your heartbeat.

Now, add words to the exhale and speak your desired manifestations into existence. This is extraordinarily powerful when you are conscious of your thoughts, words, and manifestations. To be a powerful witch or magician is to be aligned with your actions on all levels. This starts with not taking for granted that you breathe and have a heartbeat. To be infinitely grateful for each breath and each beat of your heart is to use our breath and heartbeat for success and a magical life that goes beyond that of your physical functions.

Understanding the power of clear focus, and how your breath and heartbeat consciously work in harmony on your behalf, will elevate your innate abilities of manifestation. This alleviates any known or unknown past challenges, helping you easily and joyously bring forward your heart's desires and dreams.

Now it is time to add rhythm to your rituals and ceremonies with tea.

The Power of Chants

When chanting begins with even one person saying a few words in rhythm, spoken with true intention, you can immediately feel the power of the words. When others join in, each chanting the same words in unison, the magnification of this power is undeniable.

Whether you may have been to a live sporting event or not, if you have ever experienced a crowd chanting an anthem, you know the kind of power I am speaking of. For example, when a live sporting crowd starts chanting the words to the iconic song "We Will Rock You" by Queen, it is intoxicatingly uplifting. Even if you watch a video of a crowd chanting and stomping in unison, you can't help but feel the energy of it wash over you. You may even find yourself joining in on their chant.

This rising volume of the voices, getting louder and louder, creates a cone of power; a direct action of those words is embodied by the whole crowd. Feeding off the collective energy, they give and receive energy, which amplifies even more energy. When there is more energy, that which the energy is intentionally directed at becomes illuminated. That is why chanting at a live sporting event is so effective in lifting the players up to do better, for they are feeding off the energy the chant creates.

I am not suggesting that before you drink your next cup of tea, you begin stomping your feet and clapping your hands in unison while chanting at the top of your lungs to manifest your heart's desires. Although, I cannot help but laugh at the idea of it. The point of sharing this example is that all of us have either seen, heard, or felt the power of many people chanting. This reference to a live sporting event is to underscore just how powerful of an act of creation chanting is when it is applied to your more subtle efforts with tea witchery.

The word *subtle* is key here because you do not need to be stomping your feet and chanting at the top of your lungs to elicit your own cone of power. You may correlate the power of chanting to monks in their temples praying and chanting, as they draw up energy into their words and prayers. This is an example of a more peaceful invocation of breath, heartbeat, and voice incantation.

A Tea Incantation

Incantations are a chant that have been empowered and charged with magic and Divine will. This is where a chant is transformed into a verbal spell that is spoken in rituals, over charms, amulets, and potion, such as your tea.

Reciting incantations over a cup of tea will charge it with the vibration of your words and wishes.

It can be as simple as a rhythmic repetition of the following incantation:

"As I drink this tea, I am healthy and strong."

"As I drink this tea, I am healthy and strong."

"As I drink this tea, I am healthy and strong."

Here is how to combine the incantation with your cup of tea. When chanting this incantation over your cup of tea, feel your heart beating strong. Release your breath over the cup, and charge your cup steadily repeating your chant. Visualize the vibrations of the words penetrating the tea, weaving in the life essences of your heartbeat and breath. As the tea vibrates with the highest level of healing consciousness that you have imprinted onto your healing cup of potion, it is now time to drink it in.

After performing this incantation, you are now drinking in the entire alchemical swirl of the incantation, visualization, breath, and the beat of your heart. Imbued in the essences of the tea and its qualities is the vibration of the words "I am healthy and strong" that has been charged by your breath and heart.

Savor this tea, feel this tea, and allow this tea to heal and aid the strength you asked for. You are now consuming your desires sip by sip, which you have brought into clear focus by your visualization.

"I Love You" Tea Spell

Three of the most powerful words ever spoken are "I love you." It is by design that this specific tea spell serves to powerfully bond a family. It also works to elevate and deepen the love between a couple.

When done to expand the love between a couple, I recommend both people in the relationship engage in the tea spell together. Each person creating the cup of tea for the other, so they are imbuing each other's love, breath, heartbeat, and symbol of love for one another.

When offering this tea spell to your loved one, child, or family, the words "I love you" should first be spoken by doing the following. Choose your blend of tea and then heat up the water. You can place your hand over the brewed cup of tea or teapot. Be sure to hold your hand high enough that it does not burn you. Inhale deeply and feel your heart beat three times, imprinting the rhythm onto your breath. Now release your breath in the form of the words "I love you" over the teacup or teapot. With a teaspoon serving as your magic wand, stir the shape of a heart into the tea.

This tea you are now serving is charged with the incantation and vibration of love from your words and breath. It has also been charged with the life force of your beating heart. You have affirmed this by using your magic wand to draw the shape of a heart, which is the universal symbol of love.

The sigil, symbolized by of the shape of the heart, seals in the spell in the liquid of the tea. When your loved one drinks this tea, they are literally taking in and digesting your love through the breath of your words and the vibration the tea carries in the water.

When this spell is performed to elevate the love between a couple, I recommend both people in the relationship do it together. This means each person should lovingly create a cup of tea for the other while in the physical presence of one another. This imbues the breath, heartbeat, and love for one another into the tea.

Calling in Goddesses and Gods

Each person has their own go-to goddess or god they call on for manifesting all types of desires and intentions. For some of you, though, this may be the first time you have been introduced to the process, at least in terms of its inclusion with tea. Regardless of where you find yourself in relation to calling in a goddess or god, it should be performed as an act of love and kindness.

When meditating and chanting over my tea, I will often ask for the assistance of a particular goddess or god. When I know I am going to be doing this, I will brew up a tea for myself and a corresponding tea and herbal blend to this goddess or god. I pour it into one teacup which is placed on an altar or ideal location to honor the goddess or god, and then pour the tea into my teacup cauldron. From here, I proceed to invoke them by incantation and offering of my tea.

For the purpose of this section, I am choosing a few of my favorite gods, goddesses, and deities: Blodeuwedd, Lakshmi, Green Man, and Vishnu.

Celtic Goddess Blodeuwedd

Being beautiful and glamourous has long been sought after by women and men since the beginning of time. To feel attractive and desired, beautifully Divine, and feminine has been a powerful tool of persuasion. Asking for a little help to pull these traits out from within you and project them onto your outer reality is completely acceptable and encouraged in the world of tea magic.

When it comes to calling on the qualities of beauty and glamour, I like to call upon the Celtic goddess Blodeuwedd. When I do, I offer her a cup of flower tea as Blodeuwedd literally translates to Flower Face.

Blodeuwedd was brought to life by magicians seeking to create the most beautiful women in all the land to be a match for their beloved king. This is a beautiful tale, with layers of lessons steeped in lore, imagery, and freedom. To learn more about her and other Celtic goddesses, check out the book *Goddess Afoot* by Michelle Skye.

Here is a simple yet powerful process to call on Blodeuwedd. Pour a cup of tea and place it either on an altar or wherever you see fit to honor Blodeuwedd. Next,bpour yourself a cup of tea. With a calm mind and clear focus, visualize the beauty and glamor of a goddess made of flowers. See her dancing, take her hand, and enjoy the dance with her. Inhale your tea deeply three times and exhale. Begin your chant and incantation for Blodeuwedd over your teacup. Then drink your tea.

Incantation for Blodeuwedd

Charmed beauty of loving roses.

Staying power of lavender.

I call up on you, Blodeuwedd.

To grant me beauty of flowers.

Ever staying glamour.

Legend of meadowsweet and power.

The Goddess I Am.

From head, heart, and hand.

Bless me now feminine Divine.

I accept your graces to be mine.

Blending a tea for Blodeuwedd is truly a magical experience. Since she herself was created of flower magic, it is important to honor her with as many flowers as you can. This may change with the season, depending on what is in bloom. It is often an impromptu blend and recipes will vary.

Here is a list of edible/drinkable flowers to help guide you in choosing what to brew. Be sure to check your correspondences when brewing up a pot of this beauty-enhancing tea; this will help you get all the right representations and meanings in proper alignment to help create the perfect cup of magic and beauty. Remember to be creative and add what you like along with the intentions you are seeking:

+ Rose
+ Lavender
+ Chamomile
+ Jasmine
+ Calendula

+ Heather
+ Cornflower
+ Violets
+ Pansies
+ Meadowsweet

I blend and steep in a teapot a pinch of red rose petals, a pinch of lavender, and a pinch meadowsweet. Steep for five minutes.

Lakshmi, Goddess of Good Fortune

The other goddess I call on often is Lakshmi also known as Sri. She is one of the principal goddesses of the Hinduism, known the world over as the goddess of fortune, luxury, and wealth.

When it comes to calling on the qualities of money, material fulfillment, and contentment into your life through tea, Lakshmi is an ideal source of guidance and assistance.

Incantation for Lakshmi

If you feel inclined to call on the Hindu goddess Lakshmi, here is the process I use. Please keep in mind, this process varies from time to time for me based on intentions and desires. Therefore, rather than provide a specific incantation I use with Lakshmi, I am including an incantation used by the Hindus for centuries when they call on her. This can be used as a chant, prayer, incantation, or song.

> *Beautiful goddess, Lakshmi, seated on a chariot,*
>
> *delighted by songs on lustful elephants,*
>
> *bedecked with lotuses, pearls, and gems,*
>
> *lustrous as fire, radiant as gold, resplendent as the sun,*
>
> *calm as the moon, mistress of cows and horses,*
>
> *take away poverty and misfortune,*
>
> *and bring joy, riches, harvest, and children.*

Of course, some of the specific words can be changed to suit your individual desires and intentions. For instance, you may not desire to have children at this stage of your life, so it would be wise to replace *children* with a more aligned desire.

In terms of your ritual with goddess Lakshmi, here is an easy and powerful process to replicate. When your tea is ready, pour a cup of tea and place it either on an altar or wherever you see fit to honor Lakshmi. Next, pour yourself a cup of tea. With a calm mind and clear focus, visualize an unlimited flow of prosperity and abundance flowing into your life. Feel yourself immersed in luxury and well taken care of in all ways. An important component of working with Lakshmi is to be open to receive her eternal blessings of prosperity. You deserve them and she is more than willing to help you have and enjoy all that you desire. An act of receptivity is found with inhaling your tea deeply and exhaling three times. Each time you inhale, breathe in prosperity and exhale gratitude for these abundant blessings. Begin your chant over your teacup. Then drink your tea.

Masala Chai for Lakshmi

The rich and decadent Masala Chai is a classic Indian tradition. It is perfect to honor Lakshmi. It is also available in tea bags almost anywhere that serves tea or coffee. So, if you are having a business meeting with a boss or new project manager and want to invoke the wealth and riches of Lakshmi, it can be done quickly by ordering a chai tea.

Though Masala Chai tea recipes can vary from region to region, there are a few basic traits and flavor profiles that chai tea has. Here is my recipe for chai tea:

½ cup black tea

1 teaspoon ground cinnamon

1 teaspoon ginger powder

1 teaspoon cardamom powder

1 teaspoon black pepper, coursely ground

Mix all dry ingredients in large bowl, store in airtight container, out of the warmth and sunlight. This tea is best brewed in larger batches. Place two table-spoons of mixture into large steeping bag or steeping accessory and steep it in five cups water in a pan. Place the pan onto a heater and bring the water and tea to a low boil. Reduce heat. Add one cup of milk or milk substitute. (Chocolate milk may be substituted.) Optional: one tablespoon of vanilla extract.

Tea with Green Man

Green Man, whose roots are in Pagan and Celtic lore, is a nature deity who is made of leaves and bark. He is also known as Hern of the Hunt, the Green Knight, Jack in the Green, and Grain King.

This god is a keeper of the forest and the balancer of the seasons. Green Man represents untamed nature and wild growth. He ushers in spring after winter and dances with Mother Nature who together weave a new season of spring life with lush vegetation, glorious flora, and prosperous crops which lead to bountiful harvests.

Green Man is a symbol of masculine virility, carrying with him the strength to grow and bring the forest back to life after its deep winter sleep. Green Man sows seeds and watches them bloom, which is one of the reasons he is considered a deity of male fertility.

Sharing tea with Green Man in the spring is a way to honor the cycle of new life. He can be especially helpful if you are planting a garden or doing any springtime yard maintenance, such as bush and brush removal, and tree pruning. Green Man can even assist with lawn mowing.

Incantation for Green Man

Here is a simple meditation or chant to Green Man over tea while you plan your new cycle of life, whatever you may intend for it to be. It is a particularly powerful chant when directed at your yard, land, or plants.

I give thanks to you, Green Man, and your protection of the land.

I hear your whisper in the trees.

I honor you and your presence; I feel you in the breeze.

Earth, stone, brush, and flower.

Thank you, Green Man, for sharing your growth and power.

The best way to honor Green Man is to bury your tea leaves in the earth and allow the cycle of death and life to regenerate and continue, as Green Man will feed on them directly. If you would like to share a cup of tea with Green Man, leave the tea outside for him to enjoy the scent on the air. When it is cooled, simply pour it onto the earth for him to drink.

Green Man Tea Blend

¼ cup green tea

¼ cup lemongrass

1 tablespoon horny goat weed

½ tablespoon rosemary

½ tablespoon calendula flowers or sunflower petals

Mix all dry ingredients in large bowl, store in airtight container, out of the warmth and sunlight. Brew by the cup or pot.

Tea with Lord Vishnu

Vishnu is a supreme god in Hinduism who is the preserver and protector of the universe. He appears when disorder needs to be put into harmonic balance and defends against harm and illness. For these reasons, and more, Lord Vishnu is known for governing the universe and humanity. He is the essence of all beings, the master of the past, present, future, and beyond. His divine consort and feminine balance is Lakshmi.

Sharing tea with Lord Vishnu is ideal when you are trying to build a solid foundation in your home. Lord Vishnu may also be asked to assist you in bringing harmonic balance and peace to the hearts, minds, and souls of those in your family, the ones you love, and to you.

Here is an easy-to-follow process for engaging in tea with Lord Vishnu, and an empowering incantation for him. Place a cup of tea in a sacred space or on an altar dedicated to Vishnu. Invoke this all-mighty deity with humble gratitude in your heart. Drink a cup of tea with Vishnu at the dedicated space.

Incantation to Vishnu

> *The all-pervading light of the universe. Vishnu.*
>
> *Ever-seeing jeweled eyes of the galaxy. Vishnu.*
>
> *He who spreads life and light in all directions. Vishnu.*
>
> *Lord Vishnu, enter our world, our hearts, and our minds as light.*
>
> *We will shine bright in your grace, guidance, and wisdom.*

Vishnu's Holy Tea Blend

¼ cup holy basil or tulsi

1 tablespoon chamomile

½ tablespoon jasmine green tea

1 teaspoon ginger powder

Mix all dry ingredients in large bowl, store in airtight container, out of the warmth and sunlight. Brew by the cup or pot.

Next Steps for Magical Tea Witchery

When it comes to your own visualization process, I suggest positive visions, thoughts, and dreams when enjoying your tea. I believe vibrating on a level of joy, abundance, and happiness carries the manifestation through you in the most positive and infectious way. This type of vibration makes a magnet for calling in aligned opportunities, paving a smooth and easy path to your desires and dreams to materialize in your physical reality. It also makes people around you happy and reflects to you your own inner joy.

You may find it is easier to begin visualizing what you desire by first writing down in your journal the kind of magical life you want to experience. What would you require to help make this an everyday reality for you? Remember, even if you say you want more money, a loving relationship, a new car or home, etc. the real gold in this alchemical process of manifestation is two-fold:

1. Feel into the experiences that these desires will produce for you.
2. Offer gratitude and excitement for having them in your life.

These two steps may be a stretch for you if you are fixated on what you do not have, as opposed to what you want. If that is the case, I invite you to engage in a daily practice of looking at your life and what you have through the eyes of gratitude look rather than perceiving areas of your life through the lens of lack. For if you want to call in a magical life, it starts with you living your life in magical ways right now. Nothing speeds up the material emergence of your highest desires than gratitude.

One place to begin is offering deep, genuine gratitude for your breath and your beating heart. For without both, you are not here. It goes without saying that if you want to manifest a joyous and abundantly filled magical life, you do need to be alive for this to happen.

To begin to see profound transformations in your life and the world around you, and how it relates to you, start regularly practicing being conscious and grateful for this miracle of your breath and heartbeat, which are your spark of life. From there, you can begin applying this spark of life to a new, multidimensional way of thinking, embodying, and manifesting magical experiences, such as those you engage in through tea witchery. This is where your tea practice with your Divine guides, goddesses, and gods are particularly powerful.

Chapter 7

The Magic Of Tea Leaf Reading

Tea leaf reading conjures up more than just mystical and timely messages from beyond; it also conjures your innate, inner creativity. Everyone will weave their own inner magic into a reading, making each experience unique. Although there is a lot of individuality woven into tea leaf reading, over the years a simple-to-follow system has developed.

For as creative and elaborate as you may like your tea leaf readings to be, there is still the practical preparation process required to arrive at a desired outcome. This chapter is designed to help guide you through the preparation process.

Whether you have personally experienced your own tea leaf reading, know someone who has had one, or you have given them to others, a large part of the mystery surrounding tea leaf reading is a misunderstanding about what is involved.

For instance, to many unfamiliar with the magic of tea leaf readings, the mere mention of it tends to conjure up images of a mysterious old lady in a darkened space, peering into a teacup, divining the future, and telling fortunes all from a few wet and scattered leaves sticking to the bottom of the cup. This image of tea leaf reading has been seared into the minds of most people through popular culture.

In the various ways it is shared, the story and imagery of tea leaf reading is often laced with an overt level of dismissiveness and mockery.

It was not always this way.

Tasseography

Tasseography, also known as tea leaf leading, is the art of divination or fortune-telling method that interprets the patterns in tea leaves, coffee grounds, or wine sediments that remain at the bottom of a cup from which you were drinking.

The exact origins of tasseography are hard to pinpoint. However, during the Victorian era, tasseography became quite the rage in England and throughout Europe, as a form of entertainment and a popular way of obtaining answers and clarity on all facets of life.

Despite their popularity during the late 1800s and well into the1900s, science became the predominant authority in society as to what was deemed real and what was not. As a result, tea leaf readings began being viewed as a novelty. Along with other forms of magic, the practice and proven effects of tasseography were often dismissed and mocked in mainstream conversations.

With practitioners of tea magic and its many seekers relegated to the fringes of society, the irony of the image of the mysterious old lady peering into your tea-cup was not far off, yet it was far from the whole story. Unflattering characterizations of tea leaf readings may have kept many away from satisfying their curiosity with a reading, but those who knew of its benefits were not deterred.

Those in the know would seek out tea leaf readings and trustworthy friends, or friends of friends. Some did not have to go far at all as tea leaf readings became a homegrown tradition.

The drinking of tea is already an intimate act but when you add in tasseography, and your tea leaf reading is delivered by a mother, grandmother, or close friend, the experience is amplified. In many cultures around the world there are stories that anytime there was marital strife or problems with the children, these issues were usually worked out with a cup of tea and the listening ear of a family member or friend.

So, it goes that tasseography evolved over time via a more homegrown method, as the ladies of the house would interpret their own meanings at the bottom of the cup with fortunes told, and timely guidance illuminated with a dose of women's intuition and sage advice from elders and loved ones.

The Start of Basic Tea Leaf Reading

My initial attempt doing a basic tea leaf reading turned into a giant mess. It truly is an art form that requires more than just drinking down the tea to where it is almost gone. For once you do that, now you place the saucer face-side down, over the cup while swirling it around, flip it upside down and then peer at the leaves for answers.

When I first tried doing all of that, the saucer slipped, fell on the table, and broke. The wet leaves and tea made a mess as they flew out of the cup. I looked at the cup, and only one leaf was left. I was frazzled but also amused, because here it was my first tea leaf reading and only one leaf remained. This helped ease my nerves, and I was struck with laughter.

Over the years, I picked up a few tricks of the trade. I learned that it is acceptable to use a cocktail napkin under the saucer before you place it over the cup. This will create a better grip on the cup and saucer while you flip it over. It will also catch any excess tea water and absorb it into the napkin rather than making a sloppy wet mess all over the place.

To divine using tea leaves it is best to start with a quality loose-leaf tea. Begin with either Earl Grey or a green jasmine, as they make for ideal loose-leaf tea for your readings. Although many people enjoy using bagged tea for drinking tea, keep in mind that the loose-leaf tea in bags has been processed into a fine powder. For this reason, loose-leaf tea is required for tea leaf readings.

You will want small slender leaves that will float nicely and sink smoothly to the bottom when tea is almost finished. They then stick with ease to the side of the cup when swirled and turned upside down and placed on the saucer to allow the remaining tea to drain.

After this has been done, turn the cup over and peer over the rim. Allow your mind to quiet as you focus on the leaves on the sides of the cup. Pictures and visions will start to form, so be sure to remain open and clear. Do not doubt yourself or the interpretation during the reading as it will break your concentration and your vision may fade before it is allowed to fully reveal its message.

The processes I am sharing with you in this chapter on tea leaf reading are written through examples of you giving a tea leaf reading for someone. These processes, however, work equally well for a personal reading you are doing for yourself.

Six Steps for Your Reading

Once you have chosen a loose-leaf tea, you are going to want a replicable process you can rely on, no matter the number of guests or the environment. To help you with this, here are six simple steps to frame the beautifully mysterious experience for your next tea leaf reading.

The Teacup

A solid, light-colored teacup works best. This eliminates any distraction from a pattern on the china or being able to see through clear glass. A classic teacup with a wide opening that tapers toward the bottom is preferable.

The Teacup Handle

The teacup handle is seen as the person getting the reading and it represents the now, otherwise referred to as the starting point.

The Leaves

Leaves that are closer to the handle represent things happening to the person. Leaves closest to the rim of the cup represent what is happening now. Leaves toward the bottom of the cup represent distant happenings or the past.

The Interpretation

Mentally seeing the cup as a clockface with numbers can help you interpret timing of an event by days, weeks, months, years, or hours. Depending on your interpretation it can be an indicator of an astrological sign.

The Timelines

Mentally divide the cup into four parts. This can help with seasons, directions, and element interpretations. This can also help within three months, six months, nine months, and twelve months for other valuable interpretations and timelines.

The Symbols

Interpreting symbols and their meanings is the tricky part. Symbols and meanings can be so many things for so many different people. To help, focus on symbols you are familiar with and gauge the familiarity of these symbols with your guest.

Set the Mood with Chanting

When I sit down to read tea leaves, I thoroughly enjoy the ritual, which involves the preparation. I like to have all the tea in order, cups ready and the water hot. I also chant as I am preparing for my guest(s). Chanting is not something everyone does in their preparation for tea leaf readings, so I leave it up to you to feel into whether it is aligned with your ritual and preparation.

Whether or not you are called to do chanting in your rea leaf reading, it is important to understand its purpose and benefits. Chanting helps to energetically set the mood and attune to the highest vibration in the room. Chanting also honors the elements and their relationship to the cup of tea. This further helps to create focus and align each element with a specific deity, making it easier to receive the messages from the full circle of the cup.

Here is one of my go-to chants when preparing to read tea leaves for myself and/or a guest:

> *With the plants of earth, I brew this tea.*
>
> *Water pure to guide and see.*
>
> *Caught on the air the answer steams.*
>
> *Ignited by flame are visions and dreams.*

Creating your own rituals and chants will help empower your voice and your inner eye to work in harmony together. A chant does not have to rhyme, and it can be in any form you feel guided to and are aligned with. Whatever ritual and chant you are drawn to, I invite you to just flow with it.

The Water

Better water makes a better cup of tea. A better cup of tea goes a long way toward creating a magical and tasty tea leaf reading. Therefore, it is best to use nice and clean filtered water to make tea with. Sometimes tap water can taste of chlorine, and rusty pipes certainly do not help. Of course, when it comes to tap water, a lot depends on where you live and the original source of where the water comes from. However, if all you have is tap water, then boil it up.

Pour the hot water into the cup, then place a pinch of leaves into the water. Be sure to place your hands around your cup and if you are doing a tea leaf reading for someone, ask your guest to do this with their cup. This is followed by thinking about what you or your guest would like to know and placing that information into the tea mentally. The process allows the water to vibrate, and the vibration carries the leaves. If you are doing the reading for someone else this can be done verbally too, in the form of questions and answers between you and your guest.

The vibration of the water and the simple movement of the water as the tea is being drank helps rotate and turn the leaves, absorbing the breath and wishes of the unknown to come forth into the cup.

Interpreting Stirring

When the tea is about ready to drink, inform your guest that their teaspoon is a wand and then advise them to pick up their teaspoon and stir the tea. The teaspoon is transformed into a magic wand when you intentionally visualize it as one. Ask them to think once more on what information they are seeking. In most cases, your guest will ask how to stir their tea. Answer back, "Anyway you would like to."

From here your skills of observing and interpreting will assist greatly with the reading. For while you or your guest may be contemplating what is being sought and feeling into the power of the magic wand (teaspoon), something else is occurring in the subconscious realm.

As your guest stirs their tea, there are a few things to carefully observe about their method of stirring:

+ Clockwise: People who stir in a clockwise direction are looking to bring something to themselves or to others. This stir is also associated with organization, rules, and future events.

+ Counterclockwise: To stir counterclockwise is to release or get rid of something. It is also a tell that someone is running backward and not paying attention to themselves. They are in fact unraveling or trying to fix the past.

+ Stir and Cut: A guest who stirs in a circle then cuts down the middle of the cup with the spoon is indicating they desire to put a stop to something. This is about drawing a hard line, taking sides, and not budging. This stir should be interpreted with counterclockwise and clockwise if they start with a circle stir.

+ Erratic: When the stir is a bit uncontrolled with no direction, this points to indecisiveness and impatience. It also indicates they are unsure and unclear how to take control of what they are seeking. This type of stir also routinely shows up in people who are disbelievers in the occult forms of fortune-telling.

+ Back and Forth: Stirring in a back and forth or left to right motion is an indicator of correction or starting over. In this case, they are metaphorically using the spoon as an eraser, removing what is no longer needed, and returning to a clean slate. This type of stir is also a strong unconscious motion of saying, "no."

+ Up and Down: When your guest stirs the cup up and down, this is can be interpreted as them having a strong will, or opinion. This type of stir is also the unconscious movement of the answer "yes."

+ Inside Tapping: Some guests will find themselves unconsciously tapping the inside of the cup when they stir. This can indicate they desire to be seen and heard. Sometimes, it can denote anger. Be sure to watch which of the aforementioned stirring motions the inside tapping is associated with.

- Figure Eight: Someone who stirs in the figure eight, or infinity symbol, pattern ebbs and flows with the tide and goes with the flow of their surroundings. Stirring in this motion indicates they are deeply methodical and patient. This may also be a person who is in tune with the universe and one who vibrates on a higher consciousness.

These eight types of stirring, and what they may correlate to in your guest's subconscious, are just to help you get started. For when a person is stirring it might cause you to see something else in the way they move the spoon. Therefore, it is always advised to note mental pictures, feelings, and other intuitive and psychic behaviors to apply to your reading.

This is all observation and the information you visually gather will help you better interpret the leaves for the reading.

Warm Up Your Intuition

While the leaves turn and spin in the cup after the stir, invite your guest to join you in gazing into the teacup for a minute or two. Watch the leaves float hypnotically in the cup. This is a good way to warm up your intuition and make a connection with your guest as you focus your mind and center yourself.

After gazing into the cup, invite your guest to drink their tea. While they drink their tea, you may be inclined to engage with your guest, asking questions about their experience thus far, and inquire what, if anything, they are intuiting and feeling.

When there are a few drops of tea and leaves left, ask the guest if they are finished with their tea. If so, let them know what you are about to do and then place a paper napkin and the saucer over the top of the cup, give a swirl around, and turn upside down. Turn the cup over, clear your mind, and observe the patterns of the leaves, and where they land in the cup.

The Tea Leaf Reading

Begin your tea leaf reading by staying focused, never in doubt, and remember the details from the stir. The best and truest advice anyone can share when it comes to reading tea leaves is to just say what you see. Let the pictures tell the story.

Pictures and symbols may mean many different things for many different people. It is best, then, not to get caught up in trying to remember what you read in a book regarding the meaning of a specific symbol. See the symbol, speak it, and trust it. As you speak, keep a rhythm of steady breath, and read the pictures. They all have meaning, and they all fall somewhere on the cup.

Remember to use the teacup handle as a point of now, follow the images deep into the cup, and up to the rim. The leaves will always tell you what they want you and your guest to know.

In all readings, the reader is always in control. The kind of control I am speaking of is not to suggest the tea leaf reader, be it you or someone else, should act toward your guest in an authoritative, hierarchical, or condescending manner. It means own your space, and own your gift. As I spoke to earlier in the chapter, remain focused, in the moment, and never in doubt.

Though there may be bad news and unexpected tragedies brought up from the past or seen in the future, it is important to be delicate with one's fortune and future-telling experience. I believe a good tea leaf reader will always find something positive to say to the guest, even if the message that comes through may not be what the guest wants to hear.

Reading with Flower Tea

Using flower petals can paint a much more colorful picture in the cup. You can also designate certain flowers for certain meanings. For example, red rose petals could represent love, yellow spears of calendula petals could look like spears of success, mint leaves might indicate money and wealth, yellow rose might represent a friend or friendship, and cornflowers often open and show angel wings, representing a message ffrom a loved one who has passed.

Ultimately, like a standard tea leaf reading, see it, say it, and trust it. If the rose petals tell you a story of blood because that is what it looks like to you, then say it. As with life, things are not always as they seem in a tea leaf reading. For this reason and more, it is important to relay the messages in an authentic and genuine way, for it is what your guest came to see you for, even if they have no conscious clue what was going to unfold.

You may also use flower petals with tea. This adds an extra layer of information to the symbols the leaves create.

Herbal or tisane readings follow the same general rules as a true tea leaf reading. However, there is no caffeine if that is an issue for you or your guest.

Floating Flower Divination

The floating divination is when you prepare your cup of hot water, add a few tea leaves, and then your choice of flower petals and/or herbs. You can apply the perception and art of the stir, transforming the teaspoon into a magic wand, and asking your client to stir the mix.

While the magical mix swirls and floats in the cup, ask your guest the nature of the read, even if they have already shared it. Invite them to say out loud over their cup what they are seeking. After they have spoken this aloud, allow the vibration of their words, thoughts, and desires to ripple over the water in the cup before you speak again.

To begin your reading, say what you see and keep your focus as the swirl starts to settle. In this type of reading, you will see the images change on the water as they will ebb and flow. This will create a reading that moves, which can help you see how the situation unravels or starts to happen for the guest.

As the mix of flower petals and tea leaves stills, this is a good place to have the guest take a sip of the tea and inhale the essence and experience of the reading. If the guest has more questions, you can ask them to stir the tea again. By now you know the what the intention for the reading is, and what your guest is searching for. This makes it easier to see the answers in the flowers and the leaves.

You can direct them to stir their tea again in a motion that will benefit them. Assist them in visualizing and feeling into the energy by communicating what they are creating. Again, the spoon is your magic wand and theirs as well. Empower your guest to move the vibration from the wand back into the teacup to create a more powerful outcome of their manifestation and accentuating the overall experience of the tea leaf reading.

For example, if your guest is looking to achieve a specific goal, such as being more organized or manifesting a specific outcome such as money, a new job, or a new romantic relationship, suggest to them to stir in a clockwise direction.

If they have indicated they want to be more at peace, relaxed, and/or release beliefs, behaviors, or situations that are no longer serving them, suggest to them to stir counterclockwise.

Should your guest require a specific action to be taken, to bring about any or all their desired intentions, advise them to cut the tea with a strong line. This represents drawing boundaries in a situation, which can also be done to create space for healing and elicit respect in an uncomfortable situation.

Although your guest may look to you for guidance, it is also important to provide the space and support for your guest to follow their intuition on how they should stir. This gets your guest re-involved and places their vibration and desire back into the water through the spoon. In doing so, it is also creating new pictures and thus calling on new information to come through.

As the mix floats and moves for the reading, certain parts of the leaves will fall to the bottom of the cup, while other parts of the petals will stay afloat. The parts that fell can add a deeper dimension to allow your inner eye to see what fell through, what fell back, or what should be let go of. The parts that remain on top tell their own story. It is here that the tea leaf reader weaves all these pieces together in a clear, concise interpretation for the guest to understand.

Eventually, the tea will grow cold and start to get dark and discolored. At this point, it is a good idea to wrap it up, and you and your guest can feel complete in that the leaves and flowers have given all they can.

Recipes of Herbal and Flower Teas

Concluding this chapter on tea leaf readings, I want to share with you some delightful recipes of herbal and flower teas for divining specific answers in your readings. Whether you are doing readings for yourself, family and friends, or clients, these recipes are a delicious and beautiful way to add a little kitchen witchery and magic into your readings.

Worries Be Gone Tea Blend

All herbs and flowers should be dried before use in this type of flower reading.

> ½ cup chamomile flowers and petals
>
> ¼ cup lemon balm leaves
>
> 2 tablespoons lavender flowers
>
> 2 tablespoons rose petals
>
> 1 tablespoon calendula petals

This tisane is blended with the intent of calming fears and anxieties. It is deeply relaxing and provides a beautiful swirl of floating flowers to aid in flower readings. The aromatherapeutic blend will bring a calmness to the mind while guiding a release of negativity and fear you may be having around life's peculiar situations, allowing you to relax and clearly connect mentally while you use this herbal brew for a reading.

Gently toss all ingredients together in a large bowl, then place them in an airtight container out of the sunlight.

When you are ready to use this for a reading, simply place a teaspoon of the mix onto the top of the hot water in a teacup. Allow the herbs to sit for two minutes. Then give a gentle swirling motion to the cup and begin your focus and concentration as you begin to read the petals in the teacup cauldron.

Whispering Wisdom Flower Blend

All herbs and flowers should be dried before use in this type of flower reading.

> ¼ cup lemongrass
>
> ¼ cup nettles
>
> 1 tablespoon calendula flower petals
>
> 1 tablespoon red rose petals
>
> 1 tablespoon cornflower petals

This blend gives a spectacular and vibrant visual, due to all the floating colors in the cup. The same rules apply for blending, storage, and use as the above blend. Gently toss all ingredients together in a large bowl, then place them in an airtight container out of the sunlight.

When you are ready to use this for a reading, simply place a teaspoon of the mix onto the top of the hot water in a teacup. Allow the herbs to sit for two minutes. Then give a gentle swirling motion to the cup and begin your focus and concentration as you begin to read the petals and pictures that begin to form floating in the teacup.

Allow yourself to see and interpret the floating images, there will be an array of color. Say the first things you see and trust your intuition and mind's eye.

Black and Rose:
A Tea Blend for Matters of the Heart

This tea is a lovely blend designed to use during readings about love and matters of emotions. This can be romantic love, family love, or self-love. Just as love is the most powerful and unifying emotion, roses are the universal symbol of love.

½ cup loose-leaf black tea (a single note of Chinese or Indian classic black tea, whichever you prefer)

1 tablespoon small dried red rose petals (you can find these online from herb stores or dry your own organic rose petals)

1 small pinch of coursely ground black pepper (this adds the element of protection to the heart, soothing vulnerable emotions and allowing for easier connection to truths)

1 fine mist of organic rosewater (you may also use a few drops of rose flavoring)

Mix black tea, rose petals, and black pepper in a bowl. Spread out evenly on a cookie sheet. Lightly mist the mixture of tea with a fine spray of rosewater. If using rose flavoring, place a few drops in a one-ounce fine mist sprayer bottle and fill bottle with water. Shake together and mist mixture.

For Reading with Petal Flower Tea

If your organic rose bushes produce large enough flower petals, you can cut out symbols such as hearts, arrows, rings, and moons. Press these cutouts between two pieces of parchment paper for three days. Carefully peel them off and place a few symbols in the teacup and allow them to float around to help guide your reading. This blend yields fifteen to twenty cups of tea. When you are done, be sure to store in an airtight container and keep it out of the sunlight.

Next Steps with Tea Leaf Reading

Now that you have a deeper appreciation for the magic of tea leaf reading, you may be excited to get a reading for yourself or to go out and give a reading to someone you know. Of course, if you are a professional reader, this chapter may have expanded your already deep love for the mystery of tea and the magical elements of tea leaf reading.

Wherever you find yourself at this stage of our journey together, and whatever level of experience you have with tea leaf readings, there are a few things that should be super clear by now, which will guide you along your next steps. One of the most important is to practice the art of tea leaf reading for yourself first and then try it out with others.

When I began my process of learning to read tea leaves, I figured it would be easy. I was already well adept at scrying and reading tarot cards, palms, and stones. How hard it could it be reading tea leaves? As I came to find out, like all things magical, it takes a dedicated, patient, and focused approach to create consistently desired outcomes, both for yourself and whomever you are doing the readings for. And of course, tasseography also requires curiosity and an abundance of happiness.

I practiced regularly, received some excellent guidance from those who have spent years giving tea leaf readings, and got much better at the spinning and flipping of the cup. I also learned the basics of the cup but still found myself sometimes getting hung up on the interpretations and symbols. I finally quit worrying about having to come up with dictionary-perfect definitions and meanings of the tea leaves. Once I relaxed and started to enjoy myself, I handed the process over to my intuition, and from there I got pretty good at it.

When it comes to tea leaf reading, you have learned there is much creativity and individual flare you can add to your readings. You have also learned there is a structure, flow, and process to adhere to. Not only does tea leaf reading require both the reader and the guest to be present, relaxed, and open minded, but it also helps to have a bit of experience with kitchen witchery.

Chapter 8

Charging Your Tea with Stone Energy

For as long as humans have populated the earth, there has existed a deep fascination and reverence for the multifaceted magical properties, spiritual benefits, and scientific uses of gemstones of all kinds. Some of the oldest known uses of gemstones and crystals come from ancient Sumeria, ancient Egypt, and China. These cultures, and many others, were known to include crystals in magic formulas for health, protection, and spiritual practices.

If you have ever walked in nature or visited a crystal shop, you know that gemstones and crystals find you more than you discover them. They have a distinct way of calling out to you, if you are willing to remain open and feel into their distinct energetic signatures. That is why many who work regularly with them in their spiritual and magical practices will tell you stories about their favorite crystals and gemstones. This often ranges from how they unexpectedly came across them to how their crystals and gemstones became powerful allies in their life journey.

In recent times, there has been a proliferation of gemstones and crystals, so much so that it is hard to fathom there was a time when they were not as highly sought after or valued for their magical properties and spiritual and healing benefits. Their use as powerful instruments of healing, protection, and insight into the multidimensional nature of wisdom has steadily risen in popularity as human consciousness expanded the world over.

Although often overlooked, one popular way to work with gemstones is to supercharge your tea and create your own tea gem elixir. This is an ancient practice that has since been modernized into a modern staple of tea witchery, making this chapter an essential piece of your practices with tea magic.

Tea Gem Elixirs

Adding an extra element of stone power and beauty to your tea is another magical meditation practice. This practice creates the additional balance of color, earth, and metaphysical vibration to your drink or tea potion. Doing it with tea supercharges the already natural and healing benefits of the tea and herbs.

There are gemstone elixirs, also called crystal essences, or crystal waters. These are waters that have been charged or activated by stones or a combination of stones. These waters are then used to transfer the vibrational energy from the stones into your body by drinking it or bathing in it. These elixirs have been used by healers, shamans, and witches for ages.

There are water bottles on the market today that have stones anchored into the bottle. This makes it almost automatic for you to charge and add the stone frequencies to any beverage you choose to drink. I am, not surprisingly, biased toward tea combined with stone water, which I call tea gem elixirs.

Which Stones to Use in Tea

Before you go tossing stones into your tea and drinking water, there are a few important things to know. The most important is that some stones, when combined with liquid, can be poisonous. Some might even dissolve into liquid altogether, which is not safe for human consumption at all.

The general rule for using stones in water you intend to ingest or imbue is to stay away from any stone that can leach toxins into the water. These stones are shades of blue, green, shiny, or a combination thereof.

It is important to know where your stones are coming from. Due to the increased popularity in crystals and gemstones, there are many counterfeit versions being sold as the real thing. For instance, howlite and magnesite can be dyed in many colors to imitate a variety of stones. Howlite, which is naturally white, is commonly dyed and presented as turquoise.

Agates are another popular stone that is dyed, making it harmful to put into your water and tea. Be sure to purchase your stones from reputable dealers and verify you are in fact receiving authentic stones and not a piece that has been dyed.

Stones such as malachite, lapis, and azurite contain copper that can be harmful if ingested. This includes precious stones such as emeralds, rubies, and sapphire which contain aluminum. Semiprecious stones such as moonstone, labradorite, and garnets also contain toxins that can be harmful. Shiny stones such as pyrite, marcasite, and lapis lazuli contain sulfur, which is poisonous if ingested.

Hematite does not contain a toxin. It mainly consists of iron, and iron can rust if left in water too long. When rust forms, it carries bacteria that may contain tetanus, which is harmful if it reaches the bloodstream through ingestion.

I recommend you conduct an online search to see if the stones you are attracted to are safe to use in your tea or water. Use the search phrase "Which stones are safe for gem elixirs."

There are so many stones and choices to make when you're infusing tea water with stones. First, consider the tea itself and what you are looking to get from what it is you're brewing up. Second, consider the stone and how its vibration will complement the tea. Third, consider the water you are using and if it is also aligned with your intended purpose.

Safe Crystals to Add to Water, Tea, and Gem Elixirs

+ Agate
+ Amethyst
+ Aventurine
+ Black Obsidian
+ Carnelian
+ Citrine
+ Clear Quartz
+ Jasper
+ Rose Quartz
+ Rutilated Quartz
+ Smoky Quartz
+ Tangerine Quartz
+ Tiger's Eye

Unsafe Crystals to Add to Water, Tea, and Gem Elixirs

Please be sure to thoroughly research this list of stones. I recommend these stones stay dry and be used to charge your teacups or teapots before use and not be added directly into the tea and water. If you put them directly in your dry tea, make sure they are wrapped in a natural fiber cloth before adding them into your dry tea for charging.

Remember, once you have charged your teacup or teapot with the energy of these stones you can then place the stones on the table where the cups or pot are sitting. You may even be inspired to create your own special crystal grid around the table, cups, or pot (or all three). This will continue the energetic vibration and infusion of the stones into your surroundings, your personal space, and the space in which tea is being served.

- Apatite
- Apophyllite
- Azurite
- Celestite
- Fluorite
- Gypsum
- Halite
- Hematite
- Jade
- Lepidolite
- Malachite
- Moonstone
- Opal[25]
- Pyrite
- Selenite
- Turquoise
- Ulexite

Placement of Stones

Charging your tea with the vibrational essence of the stone can be as easy as placing the stone into the box, jar, or tin of dry tea. Allow the stone energy to be absorbed by the leaves of the tea and tisanes. Speaking an incantation or chant over the stone, which can anchor your intentions and better align the magical properties and healing benefits of the stone with the tea, is a recommended practice.

---

25 Australian Boulder Opal is generally safe because it not poisonous.

Placing your stones directly into your dry tea is an ideal way to charge your tea with the energy of the stones. This is the only way you can use the energy of toxic stones that may leach out unwanted properties into the tea water.

For example, if you want to use malachite's beautiful green energy with your tea, first wrap the stone in a natural fiber such as silk, muslin, linen, or cotton. Then place the stone into your jar or tin of loose-leaf tea. If your tea is individually wrapped tea bags, there will be no need to wrap your stones first.

When you are charging your tea water by the moon, sun, or stars, there is an additional layer of vibrational power when you add corresponding stones to the water you are charging. This method of water and stone infusion can also be done at the time you are collecting your water from the elements directly.

Place the stones in the container you are collecting your water in, then place the container in the stream, river, lake, etc. This fusion can also be done if collecting water from the rain or snow, or if you are charging your tea water by sunlight.

It is not advisable to toss stones into boiling hot water. Often the stones will crack, break, and leave small dangerous shards in your teapot or cup, not to mention lose some of their potency for your charging.

Wait for the boil to cease and allow approximately nine to thirteen minutes before you add your stones. Generally, you add the tea before the stones. Your incantations may also be spoken first over the tea and water, then add the stones as the energy and ignition of the prayer.

The safest stones for this preparation are the quartz family: clear quartz, citrine, rose quartz, amethyst, and smoky quartz to name a few. These are hard and sturdy stones that will not leach toxins, and they hold up well in liquids.

You can also charge your water with stones ahead of time, then remove them before heating the water. I always recommend that when you are using your stones in this way, to ask the spark of the fire source that you intend to heat the tea water with to activate the stone energy in the water. This will brew a successful cup of stone-infused water, crystal-charged tea, or gem and tea elixir.

Six Powerful Stones

The following six popular gemstones are not only beautiful, but they are fantastic for supercharging your tea.

Clear Quartz

Clear quartz crystals are a powerful healing and energy amplifier. This is because of its structure of helical spiral crystalline from. This stone is also effective at regulating and stabilizing energy. Clear quartz crystals can be found in natural formations all over the earth. Containing a kaleidoscope of colors, clear quartz aligns, heals, absorbs, cleanses, helps with clear focus, and lends energy to all it is used with.

Clear quartz crystals can be added to the dry tea in storage or added directly to your tea water after it cools to drinking temperature.

Charging tea and tisanes with clear quartz leaves plenty of room to be creative when brewing up something special or specific. Whether you are charging teas, tisanes, or other natural remedies, because clear quartz is a universal amplifier, this stone will aid in all your tea and potion brews.

Tiger's Eye

The tiger's eye stone is safe to put directly into your tea if you desire to do so. This stone is of earth and sun and is said to bring balance and energy. Tiger's eye is praised for its protection energy for helping to ward off ill wishes someone might be aiming at you. It transmutes the power back into a balanced form emitting integrity and grounded behavior.

Tiger's eye is also good for dispelling anxiety and fear, bringing a balance of power to those who work with its energy. This stone is often associated with boosting your psychic ability and helping you to make clearer decisions in life, including friendships, career, money and much more.

Green Jade Stone

The green jade stone is one of the most prized stones of the East, as its history in China goes back thousands of years. Known to bring luck and representing wisdom, serenity, friendship, and open-mindedness, the green jade stone aligns itself with the heart chakra and helps love flow freely to friends and family.

This stone is an excellent complement to tea witchery. It can, however, be toxic if you place the stone in the water of your tea. When stored in a dry teapot or teacup, the green jade stone is perfect to use for bringing its energy to your tea and magical practices.

If you have a specific teapot you like to use when friends visit, store your jade in this pot. Allow the strength of luck, friendship, wisdom, and love of the stone or stones to vibrate into the porcelain or ceramic structure of the teapot before you make your tea in it.

After you make your tea in this pot, place the stones on the table near the tea-pot while you are enjoying the tea with your guest.

This dry storage method works great for teacups also, so you might want to have several teacups holding your stones when they are not in use.

Moonstones

A cup with moonstones will charge the teacup to aid in emotional balance, femi-nine spirituality, and intuition and will promote lucid dreaming. This cup may be the one you use when making moon water tea. In this instance, what a powerful use of the moon, as you double-charge with the water and its metaphysical stone representation. As always, choose your herbs and tea accordingly.

Labradorite

Labradorite is another beautiful stone with stunning flash and color. Although this stone can be poisonous if added directly to the water, like the other three stones I am referencing in this section, labradorite is a powerful and useful stone for charging your tea, teacups, teapots, and even the space in which you drink the tea.

Labradorite is a highly mystical stone, and it raises the consciousness and bring messages forward. It is a bringer of light and connects you with your spiri-tual and etheric body. This is a stone for intuition and dream work. This is also a stone of protection of your thoughts and dreams.

Drinking tea from a cup or pot charged with the labradorite stone will help you to align yourself with the etheric realms and access the Akashic Records.

Hematite

Hematite is an iron ore stone that facilitates protection and strength. It supports and boost self-esteem and enhances willpower. It is a useful stone to help stop compulsions and addictions. Hematite also helps on a mental scale, as it simulates concentration and focus, and enhances memory.

This stone has a strong grounding ability which is helpful when used during out-of-body experiences. It protects the soul and harmonizes the body, mind, and spirit connection.

Because hematite is beneficial for keeping someone focused, when black tea leaves are infused energetically with this stone it can help with some ADHD behaviors by bringing supreme balance and focus to the task's at hand. When added to a tea gem elixir, those who drink it will take on the energies of this stone allowing them to focus and become less scattered and more balanced.

Stone Shapes and Their Uses

The best stones for tea are smaller stones that can easily fit into a cup or a teapot. Larger stones may be used in large jars to charge the water first. The larger stones can be used directly in the large jars when making sun tea.

Swallowing a gemstone can be dangerous and harmful and can cause a choking hazard. If you are preparing tea for guests, and charging this tea with stones, be mindful to tell your guests so that there are no surprises if they find a stone in their cup.

It is important to make sure that you wash your stones in clean water before you use them in tea that you plan to drink. For best results, use cold water, and add in salt if you can. Also, do not use soap to clean your stones. There are many benefits to cleaning your stones, one of which is to clear away all dust and germs that may have settled on them. Washing them is also beneficial for clearing away any unwanted metaphysical residue off them as well. As a rule, most stones should be cleansed before each use, no matter what you are using them for.

Single-Point Wand

A crystal that contains a point at one end is ideal to be used as a wand. Using the point, it can also draw out negativity or emotional or mental blocks away from the persons. This stone can also point and lend new perspective, delivering timely guidance when you are searching for answers. This crystal can direct energy from the point of the stone into the tea or teapot, acting as a conduit for direct infusion of energy into the tea.

Double-Pointed Crystal or Double Termination

These are crystals with points at both ends. This type of stone radiates and channels energy from both ends, making it a stone of balance. This stone can also act as a bridge to connect the physical world to the spiritual world. It is also known to give a boost of physical energy when you are exhausted.

Phantom Crystal

This crystal appears to have a ghostly crystal inside another crystal. This occurs over millions of years of formation. This stone helps to put the past into perspective and facilitates learning, understanding, growth, and evolution. This stone can also be helpful when dealing with people, especially helpful in better understanding family members.

Crystal Spheres

These are usually shaped by humans from larger crystals. When using them for tea, choose spheres that are small, such as the size of a large marble. Placed in a teapot this shape allows the crystal to emit as well as draw in energy from all directions. Crystal spheres are helpful in allowing the user to see nonlinear answers from the past as well as the future. For this reason, crystal spheres are the preferred shape used by scryers or seers for fortune-telling.

If you are having tea with a friend and you want to catch up on important things or just all things relevant to your lives, place a sphere-shaped crystal into your teapot. This will help guide the conversation and lead to open sharing of information.

Egg-Shaped Crystals

These too are shaped by humans and do not form this way naturally. Egg-shaped crystals can help realign the physical body, making them ideal choices for healing and releasing illnesses. This shape also represents fertility and femininity and can be helpful when carrying a child or preparing the womb for a child.

Record Keeper Crystal

This crystal is helpful when studying or learning new information. You will know a record keeper crystal by how its crystal has definite triangles on the side or at the point. This crystal is a meditation crystal that can help you to unlock spiritual knowledge and open doors to past lives. Record keeper crystals are a facilitator of inner exploration of forgotten wisdom, making this stone ideal to use when seeking the knowledge of the Akashic Records.

Soulmate Crystal

You can recognize a soulmate crystal by how it appears to have two stones growing side by side. This is a crystal of relationships, partnerships, and friendships, and is not relegated to just romantic unions. The closer the stones are in size the more harmonious the relationship will be. The soulmate crystal can help to bring a partnership to you, heal a partnership you are already in, or keep your partnership strong and healthy.

Heart-Shaped Stones

These are another set of stones shaped by humans. Even so, heart-shaped stones work well symbolically when matters of the heart and deep connections are being worked with. Consider which stone the heart is cut from and apply those principles to your work.

Use rose quartz or heart-shaped stones in your tea when you are speaking of love or matters of the heart. They can also be used to charge your tea when you are seeking to heal broken hearts or help bring into focus the kind of love you or someone you are working with in a reading is seeking.

If you or someone you're having tea with is searching for a relationship, I suggest using rose quartz and a soulmate quartz crystal in your teapot to help bring into focus the kind of partnership or lover that is being sought after.

When doing tea leaf readings, it can be helpful to drop a small, single-point crystal into the teacup that is being drank out of. The point can help focus the reading to necessary answers. This is mostly to help the person being read for, as it can assist them in seeing the answers for themselves.

Most quartz crystals can be added to the teapot when the tea has cooled to just above drinking temperature.

Adding Stones

In this section, you will learn about additional variations of clear quartz, in this case, amethyst, rose quartz, and citrine, along with recipes and some incantations when you work with these stones to supercharge your tea, in this case—sun tea!

Sun is fire, tea is water, and the clear quartz is earth. When they are brought together outside in the open air to brew and blend, a whirl of energy is yours and/or your guests' to ingest. This charged sun tea will spark clear-thinking and add an energetic zing to those who drink it. Remember to rinse your stones off with water before using them to remove any unwanted dust or energies that may have attached to them.

Earl Grey Tea and Clear Quartz

Prepare this tea with clear intent to uplift, bring focus, and energize the day. You will need eight tea bags to a gallon or ¼ cup loose tea in an infuser. Place stones in a gallon container to facilitate clear thinking and charge the tea with the highest level of aligned energy balance. Fill the container with water. Invite in the flowing energy of water to move through and carry into you and to those who drink this tea the purest vibration of the stones, the clarity of their energy, and the purity of the water. Add the Earl Grey tea (see page 36). This tea is already aligned with uplifting qualities and the healing anti-depressant oils of bergamot. Invite the happiness and joy from the bergamot to be supercharged by the water, which in turn is being energized by the stones. Cover, then place outside in the sun for one to three hours. The time is dependent on how strong the sun is and how hot the day is. Be sure to taste-test to determine you reach the desired strength and flavor you are looking for.

If you are thinking ahead to making this as an iced tea, try adding a leaf of mint or lemon balm to your ice cubes in the ice tray before freezing. This gives an extra boost of flavor, refreshment, and beauty to your glass of iced sun tea, while introducing the element and correspondences of the herbs in the ice into your brew.

Rose Quartz and Healing Heart Tea

Rose quartz crystals are for all matters of the heart. This can include love for yourself, love for another, or family and friendship love. This is the stone of infinite love and peace.

Rose quartz and tea can help to heal a broken heart. These stones can be added to the dry tea in storage or can be added directly to your teapot once the tea has cooled. Here is what you will need:

½ cup black tea

2 tablespoons red rose petals

2 teaspoons cardamom seeds

½ teaspoon rosemary

3 small rose quartz stones

Blend all ingredients together in container with a lid. Add the three rose quartz stones one at a time. (1 rose quartz) to represent the healing of the mind and easing of the tears. (1 rose quartz) to represent the healing of the heart and to steady its beat. (1 rose quartz) to represent the healing of the spirit and the joy that is ready to shine through and rise. Store in an airtight container out of the sunlight. Brew your cup or pot of tea as usual. When holding this hot cup of healing heart tea, inhale deeply the calmness of the cardamom and the softness of the rose, catching an uplifting touch of rosemary. Then exhale all the worry and pain your heart has been feeling, your mind has been seeing, and your spirit has been dragging around. Repeat the deep breaths and inhale the steam from the tea, filling your lungs and senses with the calmness of the brew. Then, exhale and release the weariness. Take as many deep breaths as you need, keeping clear your intentions of putting your heart back together and realigning your body, mind, and spirit.

If this is a tea for your guest be sure to reference what they are inhaling and exhaling.

Repeat over the next few days to a week, or until you have finished all the tea you made. When you are done, remove the rose quartz stones from the jar and rinse them in cold water, clearing off energetic residue and place them somewhere safe. They can also be carried with you in a mojo bag, purse, or your pocket.

Amethyst and Peaceful Sleep Tea

The amethyst stone enhances spiritual awareness and helps to stop psychic attacks against you. Amethyst is a powerful stone for mental calmness and can facilitate mental clarity and promote intuition and psychic gifts. This stone is also useful when guarding against nightmares and negative thoughts. Amethyst is commonly associated with your third eye chakra, making this helpful when working to open your third eye or align and balance your crown chakra.

I recommend using an amethyst stone to be used in tea gem elixirs that benefit all mental and psychic clarity work. I also recommend the stone to be used to supercharge tea gem elixirs to ease nightmares and clear the mind for peaceful and restful sleep. Here is what you will need:

½ cup of peppermint

¼ cup catnip

2 tablespoons chamomile

2 tablespoons lemon balm

1 tablespoon passionflower

1 amethyst crystal

1 clear quartz single point crystal

Blend all herb ingredients together in container that has a lid.

Incantation for Peaceful Sleep Tea

> *With this tea I peacefully sleep—A restful night I shall keep.*
>
> *No dreams of terror will I wake—A peaceful, restful, night I take.*
>
> *With this stone I calm my mind. (Add the amethyst to the dry tea)*
>
> *Peaceful dreams this night I find. (Add single-point quartz to dry tea)*

Drink a cup or two of the peaceful sleep tea about one to two hours before bed. With each sip inhale deeply the aroma and warm steam, allowing it to clear your senses. The aroma of the herbal therapy activates the synapses in your brain and will ease you into a comfortable and relaxed state, properly preparing you for a peaceful sleep.

Sweet Dreams

This is a recipe that is especially helpful for children or for people who struggle with nightmares. Here is what you will need:

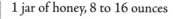

1 jar of honey, 8 to 16 ounces

1 amethyst stone

1 double-pointed quartz crystal

Incantation for Sweet Dreams

> *With this stone I calm my mind. (Add the amethyst to the jar of honey)*
>
> *Sweetened dreams this night I find. (Add double-point quartz to the jar of honey)*
>
> *To clear a path I use these stones, so that all the nightmares leave me alone.*

This honey is now charged and ready to use as a nightly ritual before bed. It can be added to tea or simply enjoyed by the spoonful.

If you are preparing the Sweet Dreams tea for a child, or even an adult, I recommend you involve them in the process, especially with the incantation. Keeping this interactive provides them the space to feel empowered, which helps ease their restlessness at night. Also, making tea and speaking incantations is fun, so this helps them go to sleep with a smile on their face.

Lemon Joy Green Tea with Citrine

Citrine is a beautiful, bright golden to orange-colored stone. It is a facilitator of energy and carries the power of the sun. This is a stone of happiness and creativity, holding the power to attract abundance, prosperity, and wealth.

This stone can also help to boost your confidence and remove self-destructive tendencies. Additional powerful properties of citrine include improving motivation, self-expression, and facilitating a positive attitude. Overall, citrine is a high-energy stone and carries a drive and uplifting motivated force with it. This tea will bring joy and confidence to those who drink it. The lemon joy green tea with citrine is a successful addition to any workday because it motivates you and opens you up to being receptive to the flow of abundance and prosperity. Here is what you need:

> ½ cup of dragonwell green tea (or your favorite green tea)
>
> 1 tablespoon of lemongrass
>
> 1 teaspoon lemon verbena
>
> Upon brewing use a fresh wedge of citrus rind, either lemon or orange only (your choice)
>
> Citrine stone

Bring water to a boil then remove from heat and let stand for five to seven minutes. Place one tablespoon of green tea mixture, one fresh lemon wedge, and one citrine stone into a three-by-five-inch muslin steeping bag and then place in teapot. You can also place herbs and citrine stone into a pot with a steeping basket. Pour the water over the mixture and allow it to steep for about three to five minutes.

Enjoy and share this delicious brew of motivation and joy with yourself and others. This is a great pot of tea to make at the workplace when you are trying to get your coworkers or employees on the same page and excited about what they are doing.

Remember to store your lemon joy green tea with citrine mixture out of the sunlight to use on another day.

If you would like it iced, steep the tea longer (eleven to thirteen minutes) and allow it to cool, then pour over ice. Allowing it to steep longer brings up a stronger flavor so when you add the ice it will not dilute the taste of this powerfully uplifting gemstone tea elixir.

A Cup of Tea to Catch a Liar

If you're trying to get to the bottom of something, where the truth has eluded you, or you feel like someone is lying to you, I suggest serving oolong tea charged with a pyrite stone. Place a piece of pyrite stone that has been wrapped in silk in the box, jar, or tin of dry tea that you are planning to serve your guest.

Pyrite is also known as fool's gold, and carrying a piece of pyrite may help you to see through lies. By placing the stone in the tea, be mindful that you are seeking the truth from the person drinking the tea.

> **IMPORTANT:** *Do not put a pyrite stone in the tea water. Pyrite releases toxic metalloids in water that are harmful for human consumption. Akin to lies and deception, pyrite can be toxic if consumed.*

Oolong is a tea with a curing and drying time that falls between a green and black tea. In tea witchery, this represents the in-between space. This makes it the perfect cup of tea to share with someone who you are seeking truth from. This is because it frees them from one side or the other and allows them to easily speak truth in your presence, all the while sharing a great tasting cup of tea. *Be careful what you say, for it will work on you, too.*

Your Next Steps with Stones

With so many gemstones, teas, and herbs, the magical concoction of potions and healing elixirs are endless. When you are working with stones in your tea witchery practices, be sure you do your own research and keep yourself safe. Most of all, have fun layering your correspondences and keep your intent clear and focused.

For your next steps, as always, I recommend you put into practice what you have learned. Here are five next steps you can take with stones and tea witchery:

1. As you begin to work with charging your tea with gemstones, take time to revisit key sections of this chapter for additional review.

2. Begin working with gemstones that you are attracted to, in terms of both their look and feel. Despite their generalization in terms of properties and definitions, gemstones and crystals are highly personal, so be sure to look up their distinct magical properties and spiritual and health benefits beyond what I provided you here. As with most things, it's best to experiment with the stones and teas to find the right combination for your purpose, whether you are meditating, scrying, or healing.

3. Explore ways to work with gemstones beyond tea witchery, such as holding them, and even strategically placing them in areas in your home, such as altars and grids.

4. Get a book about stones, their meanings, and their purposes. There are a great many on the market, and you can also get started by searching online for the meanings and purposes of gemstones and crystals.

5. Whether you are new to gemstones and crystals, or you have enjoyed a long love affair with them, always be sure to purchase your stones from reputable dealers and verify you are in fact receiving authentic stones and not a piece that has been dyed.

I want to conclude this chapter with sincere and loving gratitude to the gemstones for the vibrational work they have done for me personally and professionally. This practice of gratitude is something I highly recommend you do for the gemstones you personally work with, and those individuals you may be called to work with through gemstones.

Gemstones reciprocate the energy of gratitude. Having gratitude and appreciation for the sturdiness of these earth treasures helps to align you and your connection with the stones. This will bring even further harmonious workings to you and the stones while you enjoy your teapotions and gem elixirs.

Chapter 9

Sigils, Symbols, and Tea Magic

How do you communicate the multidimensional nature of universal laws of creation and manifestation throughout time to different cultures, each of whom speak different languages, and have different interpretations of life? The answer is through sigils and sacred symbols.

Sigils and sacred symbols have served as an interpretive bridge to communicate between the unseen worlds and our own physical reality since the beginning of time. In place of words, a sigil can embody the energetic signature, spirit, and intentions of both human and non-physical beings.

Think of sigils and symbols like access codes to a computer, that when understood and applied in specific ways, they can unlock powers and access to other worlds previously unknown to humans. To work with this diverse level of magical power requires respect, responsibility, and good stewardship of one's intentions for manifesting or summoning deities and desired outcomes through sigils.

While much of today's magical practice of using sigils and sacred symbols have their origins in the Middle Ages, their use is as vast and unique as the many cultures are that have applied them over many thousands of years. Even the letters in our names could be considered as sigils. When we combine these sigils together to create our name, this is a form of magic as it contains the ultimate spark of who we are.

The term *sigil* comes from the Latin word *sigillum*, meaning *seal*. Although the practice of using sigils and sacred symbols has been ongoing throughout human history, it underwent a series of changes during the 1800s and early 1900s. Influential groups and occult artists of that era, such as the Hermetic Order of the Golden Dawn and Austin Osman Spare, contributed to a resurgence and interest in the ancient practice of ceremonial magic with sigils and sacred symbols that swept across Europe, eventually making its way into modern-day usage.

Over the years, I have worked extensively with sigils and sacred symbols, incorporating them into my tea witchery practices. For this chapter, I am going to share with you some basic rules for stirring the spiral symbol into your teacup or teapot. You will also learn how to amplify the power of your tea magic with sigils through incantations for healing, health, and calling success to you. In addition to this, I will share with you how to forge your own sigil or personal symbol, along with how to align your tea and herbs properly with your desired outcome, while working with sigils.

Transform Your Teacup into a Cauldron

Using sigils and sacred symbols in your tea magic practices is an immensely powerful way to align your intentions and your tea. This practice of stirring in sigils and symbols ultimately transforms your teacup into a cauldron.

A sigil is a seal, a painted symbol, or drawing said to have magical power. One of the most universally recognized sigils is that of a drawn heart. A heart represents love of some kind, making it a universal sigil that speaks a universal language that people from all corners of the world can understand.

If you were to serve your family a cup of tea, stirring in a heart shape before handing it to them would seal in the symbol of love. Upon them drinking in the tea, they would be receiving the love of the collective magic that is held in the shape of a heart that has been stirred into the tea.

Using the Spiral Sigil

Of all sigils, none are as ubiquitous as the spiral. One of the more complex and well-known spirals is the triskelion, which is a triple spiral found in artifacts dating back to the Neolithic and Bronze ages. It is most prominently associated with Celtic traditions. With such power attributed to the spiral sigil, it is not surprising it has been used to induce hypnotic trances, as it symbolizes the consciousness of nature in the way a flower blooms.

For example, when you look at a spiral sigil, and that of a blossoming flower, you can see that from its center the shape and flow of energy begins within and expands outwardly. This is likened to the spiral nature of the cosmic universe, which is often referred to as the Fibonacci Spiral or the Golden Spiral.

The spiral nature of energy has its ebbs and flows in the way one's life can unfold. For example, there are conjured images of Divine spiral staircases with one's higher self in their glorious ascension, representing a higher state of awareness. The opposite can be found in human experiences when you or someone you love is caught in the middle of a downward spiral, where they are descending into a less than pleasant emotional state.

For these reasons, when using the spiral symbol in your tea magic be sure to understand the nature and intention you are using it for as the direction of a spiral can represent vastly different sets of energies. Here are two basic rules for stirring the spiral into your teacup or teapot:

1. Clockwise spiral is used to draw things in toward you and to protect.
2. Counterclockwise is used to release, let go of, and banish.

Seven Tea Magic Sigil Spells

Here are seven tea magic spells using sigils.

Interlocking Name Sigil

Draw the initials or names of two lovers in the center of the teacup with a heart symbol stirred around. This is to imprint and surround the couple with the protection of love.

Lovers Incantation over Teacup

> *We are surround by love. Everlasting, ever strong,*
>
> *We are protected by love, our heart is one.*
>
> *Nothing can harm us, no one can divide us. Everlasting ever, strong.*

Square of Stability

Stir a square into your teacup, at each corner a corresponding letter to represent the directions of north, south, east, and west. This represents foundation and strength in your home. You can add your initials or stir your name in the center to represent self-stability.

You can also use the interlocking name sigil of you, your spouse, and your children to create a stable home environment.

Four Corners of This Home Incantation over Teacup

> *From the east I call the whirling winds to sing songs of joy.*
>
> *From the south I ask for energy and flames of creativity.*
>
> *From the west I call the life force of water to balance and nourish.*
>
> *And of the north I ask for your strength of rock and earth to hold steady this home and hearth.*

Third Eye Enhancement

Draw an eye symbol in your teacup to keep you focused on your dreams. This will allow you to clearly see the visions you possess. This is especially helpful when reading tea leaves or scrying with your tea.

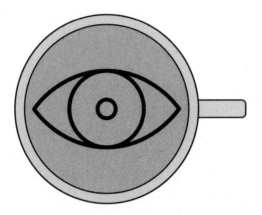

Psychic Vision Strength Incantation over Teacup

Visions strong and visions clear, open my eyes to what is near.

Show me truth and guide my sight, illuminating what lurks in twilight.

Clockwise Spiral

The clockwise spiral is used to draw energy, thoughts, entities, things, and successes to you. The handle of the teacup represents you; begin your stir here, ending in the center of the cup. While you stir say your incantation or chant over your teacup. Start with your spoon or wand, at the handle of the teacup. Moving along the outside of your cup (but not touching the cup) in clockwise direction continue to stir the circle slowly to the center of the cup. Gently tap the tip of your spoon or wand in the bottom center of the cup.

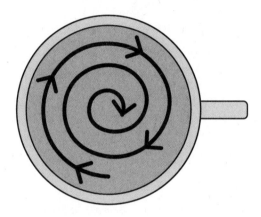

Success Incantation over Teacup

> With the intentions of success, I draw to me, all things I have asked
> for I now see.

> Swirling spiral of synchronicity, with great successes I imbue this tea.

Healing and Health Incantation over Teacup

> Health and well-being, I draw to me, strength and healing I now see.

> Strong and sturdy as earth and tree, in perfect health I imbue this tea.

Counterclockwise Spiral

The counterclockwise spiral is used to release negativity, bad habits, and old thought patterns, and to remove these things which bring you down. Starting in the center of your cup with your spoon or wand, begin to unwind what no longer serves you. Erase and let go of these things with the counterclockwise spiral. You will want to end at the rim of your teacup on the direct opposite side of the teacup handle.

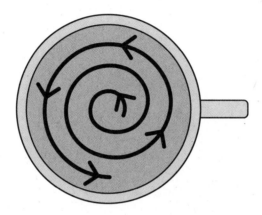

Releasing Gossip, Trash Talk, and Lies Incantation over Teacup

> *All negative chatter, gossip, and lies. You are released, I say goodbyes.*
>
> *Whispering winds there is a change, from these endeavors I refrain.*
>
> *True to myself and my tea I remain.*

To Stop the Wrong Incantation over Teacup

This incantation is intended to stop someone from doing you harm or wrong, be it a co-worker, family member, or friend. This works best if you can use the counterclockwise spiral and incantation over the teacup they will be drinking out of ahead of time.

> *Stop it now and let me go.*
>
> *You have no power don't you know?*
>
> *Release it now and put it down, in this tea all negativity is drowned.*

Invoking Sigil

This formal sigil in your teacup should be used for ritual tea and potion brewing. Using the five points of the star, set within the cycle of the full moon (your teacup), you can use the invoking pentagram to enhance the power and magic that you are practicing with a group or in a solitary setting.

This teacup sigil should be ushered in with the calling of the directions and elements.

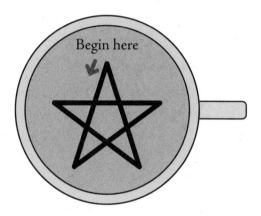

Directions and Elements Incantation over Teacup

> *From the north I call upon the guiding light of the northern star.*
>
> *From the south I call upon the spark of flame to ignite this request.*
>
> *From the east I invite the whispering winds and voices to be heard.*
>
> *From the west I honor you in the nourishing water of this tea.*
>
> *As it is above in the star lit sky, set within the perfect circle of this teacup.*
>
> *As it is below in the earth where the roots of tea and ideas grow.*
>
> *Thank you for the strength and blessings as the portal of this teacup is open.*

Banishing Sigil

As with the invoking sigil this symbol is a formal practice used in coven work and solitary practices. It too should be used in conjunction with calling in the energy of the elements and directions. The banishing sigil is one that will help you rid and cleanse yourself or those in a coven of bad habits, negative attachments, and unnecessary entities.

Begin here

Banishing Incantation over Teacup

> *From the east I call upon the winds of change.*
>
> *From the south I call upon the renewal of fire.*
>
> *From the west I honor the cleansing force of water.*
>
> *From the north I give gratitude for your strength of stone.*
>
> *As it is above in the ever-expanding cosmos of enlightenment.*
>
> *As it is below the core of molten lava, minerals, and metals.*
>
> *Be here now to aid in the release and banishment of burdens and troubles.*

Make Them Your Own

As with all intuitive-based magic and incantations, I invite you to make them your own. Add a few words here, more details and specifics there. The closer your words and desires are in alignment, the clearer the vision and intent becomes, and the more directed is the vibration of your tea. This allows your body to vibrate on the highest frequency that you have tuned your intentions in to as you drink in your tea.

The same goes for how you like to drink your tea. If you like your tea sweet, add in honey, agave, maple syrup, or even sugar if you desire. Stir in a spiral motion into your teacup or teapot to spike your tea spells and incantations with a blast of sweetness.

You can use simple chants alone in your tea by just adding the sweetness in and saying a chant or prayer of your choosing. You can also combine this with other tea sigil and incantation work to build a stronger and more layered, teacup cauldron spell.

Try drawing your sigils, symbols, and sacred marks with the actual honey, agave, pure maple syrup, or simple syrup. This allows the impression of the mark to be in the sweetness itself. Therefore, when you chant over this it will also carry the vibration in the mark and the sweetness, leaving the person drinking the tea satiated in thoughts of the sweetest intent.

Sweet Tea Incantation

> Sweet successes golden honey, flow to me as endless money.
>
> Agave nectar sweet and pure, bringing forth the perfect cure.
>
> Maple tree let your sweetness flow; your syrup of knowledge helps me grow.
>
> Sugar crystals sweet Divine, grant my wishes and make them mine.

Using Your Own Sigils and Symbols

Another ancient practice of working with sigils and symbols is creating your own and applying them in amulets, talismans, and yes, even your tea. Forging your own sigil or personal symbol can hold a great deal of power and intention.

For example, let us start with imagining you have just blended and brewed up a very personal and unique teapotion using of all the right flowers and tea. You have used the right, specific water, charged by the light of the moon or the time of the sun on your day of the week. You then stir in your initials into your cup, sealing the spell and tea potion with a final signature of your power, intent, and craft.

If you are working with a coven, a friend, or family member, you can combine your initials to make a blended symbol. This sigil will use the strength and power of all involved, creating an energetically entwined, dynamic seal of directed intent.

Applying the Sigil

Whether it is your own sigil or part of a blended symbol, a sigil can be stirred into the teacup or teapot. They can also be drawn onto the teapot or teacup with a marker or sacred paint. You can use a paint brush and use the tea itself to draw with. You can also draw the sigils inside the teapot or teacup with honey or agave, or even sugar water.

The sigils can be drawn with an altar tool such as a wand, or an athame. You can use your finger to draw onto the teapot, teacup, or the teacup saucer.

Another unique and powerful sigil is one that combines your name and your lover's name. This is a way to build a stronger and more unbreakable bond between each other. This works best if those involved in the relationship create the sigil together. Once you have created this sacred symbol you can begin using it in your tea magic and potion imbuing.

Draw the symbol in the teacup, and from there draw a heart around it to keep you surrounded by love. When used in your first cup of morning tea, this is a great way to start your day and strengthen your bond and renew your vow in one simple cup of tea magic.

If you enjoy a nice relaxing herbal tea before bed you can apply the same stir here as well. Draw in your sacred symbol that represents those in the relationship, and draw a heart around it to keep you protected by love while you sleep.

This combined symbol also works well when applied to sex magic and fertility teas and tea spells. First, you will want to align your tea and herbs properly with your desired outcome. After this is completed, applying your sigil is next.

Stir the clockwise spiral in your teacup or teapot to welcome new life or to draw in and hold your relationship's love, passion, desire. Make sure you end your spiral at the handle of the cup or pot, for the handle represents you and/or the intent. Now, add your combined sigil to the top of the spiral to seal in your desires. Drink the tea together.

Next Steps with Sigils

Like many of the magical practices and divination tools I have referenced throughout this book, I invite you to follow your inner guidance and curiosity on what resonates with you in terms of sigils and sacred symbols. In this case, if you wish to weave in sigils and sacred symbols with your tea witchery, you can build on your knowledge by looking into books, documentaries, and courses dedicated to the use of sigils and sacred symbols in the practice of Divine magic.

For those of you who are interested in tea parties that are centered around sigils and sacred symbols, you can begin exploring your own tea party kits. This has become quite popular in recent years and is something many of my customers have started doing.

Whatever you feel called to in your ongoing journey with tea witchery, the great thing about sigils and sacred symbols is that whether you use one you know of or make your own, be sure to align your intentions with the proper tea blend that corresponds to your desired outcomes. From there, whatever sigil you apply to your tea or teacup cauldron, you know it is activated and infused with the highest and most genuine of vibrations.

Chapter 10

Tea Magic and Spirit Communication

A gentle touch, a cool brush of wind, and the familiar smell of a loved one hangs in the air. If you have experienced this, only to look around with your body's eyes and see nothing, there is a good chance you have encountered the presence of the spirit world. These are not random occurrences that can be shrugged off, which is why when they do occur, your skin suddenly ripples with goose bumps. If the energy you feel is a familiar one, you may find yourself awash with a flood of memories of a loved one. For example, to feel the warm caress of your grandmother's smile, which nearly stops your heart with joy and remembrance—this is not an uncommon experience, nor is it unnatural to communicate with spirits.

Your logical mind may try and persuade you to look past these experiences, but your inner being knows better. At one time or another, I believe we have all had encounters with the spirit world. As much as some would like to think of it as unnatural, communing with the spirit world is a natural part of being human.

These interactions with the dead are easy to pick up on and for many, they are easy to shrug off. Some people, however, have a stronger and more open connection with the spirit realm. For them, it seems they are a beacon of light for lost spirits wandering through the unknown darkness between the worlds of form and the formless. Whether these spirits are hoping to feel life again, looking to get a timely message to a loved one, or simply seeking a way to find closure and move into a higher dimensional state, the interaction between the dead and the living is alive and well in the modern age just as it was thousands of years ago.

What Is Spirit Communication?

Spirit communication, which is also referred to as necromancy, is an ancient practice of Divine magic that revolves around conscious interaction with the dead or non-physical spiritual entities. The purpose of spirit communication is to summon the energetic signature and spirit of a loved one, relative, or spiritual being that you seek to receive answers from. The answers being sought are unique for each person, but generally speaking, they pertain to a specific question or issue you are facing. Sometimes, you do not even have to be clear on the question or issue, but simply be open to the message from the dead.

The word necromancy, like many words in our modern age, is derived from both Latin and Greek. In Latin it is the word *necromantia*, and in Greek *nekromanteía*. Necromancy has origins in benevolent magic. This has led many to perceive it as both unnatural and of a dark, evil nature, when in truth, it is neither.

A Sacred and Cherished Practice

When practiced with love, respect, and mindfulness, there is nothing sinister about spirit communication. There are many ways to summon the spirit world into your physical presence. For this chapter, I will share with you how to use tea magic and spirit communication.

Spirit communication has been a sacred and cherished practice of many cultures for good reason. There is much joy, wisdom, and fulfillment that can and does often come from mindfully interacting with the dead. For myself, personally and professionally, I have practiced spirit communication for many years, as is the case for many witches and necromancers that I know.

I have witnessed the unimaginable burden of eons of suffering peacefully reconciled for people in one reading with the dead. I have also observed beautiful lessons and inspired wisdom shared from the spirit world that have positively transformed lives with readings I have facilitated for others, and those that have been done on my personal behalf.

For this chapter, I am going to share with you what to look out for when interacting with the dead, the preferred type of teas that will aid with communicating with the dead, and incantations to use as a vibrational bridge when speaking with the spirit realm. I'll also go over precautions and protective measures to take when calling on spirits in the underworld, how to set up and facilitate a tea party for the dead, and a real-life cautionary tale about what to do and not do when you have a gift for communicating with spirits.

You will also learn how to communicate with spirits through a safe and enlightening process involving tea parties. For those who are new to tea parties with the dead, you may be surprised there is such a thing. More than a current trend, tea parties with the dead are an ancient tradition, and fill an important and enjoyable role in tea witchery.

Please keep in mind, this is a chapter about spirit communication in a book about tea magic. There are many wonderful books dedicated entirely to the spiritual and magical practice of working with the spirit world. I say this because I do not want anyone, whether you are being introduced to spirit communication for the first time, or you are well trained and acquainted in the art form of communing and communicating with the dead, to mistake the intention or content of this chapter to be a definitive guide to spirit communication.

No matter where you find yourself in terms of experience with spirit communication, my intention here is to provide you a grounded place to begin working with tea magic and spirit communication. If you are an experienced practitioner of necromancy, may this chapter serve as a refreshing and important reminder for you of both the dangers and the joys of facilitating readings with the spirit world.

Dancing with the Dead

Individuals who have a powerful connection with spirits must take great care and be mindfully cautious when dancing with the dead. It is one thing to invite an ancestor of your own to partake in a cup of tea with you, be it calling upon the spirit of a grandmother, grandfather, or beloved relative who has passed on. These spirits are easy to call on when you have a direct connection to them. In these scenarios, a cup of tea, a favorite memory, marigold flowers, or other personal mementos you may have that the spirit might have an affection for serve as an effective instrument for bridging the two worlds.

The spirit of a relative or beloved who crosses back over to engage with you rarely means harm. In general, they deliver direct messages, help you locate lost items, lend timely guidance, help protect you, and they bring an overall sense of helpfulness. Overall, these spirits share a friendly and loving vibration.

Then, there are other less friendly spirits. These spirits represent a lot of different intentions and are not always of human origin. For instance, there is the wandering spirit who is lost and simply wants to connect but has little concern for the effects of their intrusion. These kinds of spirits are generally harmless but can be both annoying and jarring to those who have little experience interacting with the dead.

Then you have people who passed on who were not kind in their waking life and are even less so in their non-physical state. Examples of these kind of spirits include those who are both intrusive and abusive, many of whom seek a host in the living world to satisfy a penchant for human addictions and afflictions.

For example, imagine a person who was once living, who was addicted to alcohol and food with high sugar content. Perhaps they died because of too much of both. Well, if that spirit has not crossed over into the peaceful afterlife, they may seek out unwitting hosts in the world of the living to continue their insatiable appetite for alcohol and sugar. In this example, they can attach themselves to a living being, and before that person knows what has come into their field of energy, they are unknowingly drinking excessively, consuming unhealthy foods, and finding themselves behaving or living in highly destructive ways.

When dark attachments occur, such as the general but common example above, it is not only disruptive and unsettling for the person whose life has been hijacked, but it can be highly disruptive for family, friends, and coworkers, all of whom have no idea where the person they loved and knew has gone.

Now, the example of a spirit addicted to alcohol and sugar who takes over a living host to get their daily fix may seem humorous if placed in a comedic movie; it is, however, a very real and highly dangerous circumstance. There are countless real-life examples of this happening to people all over the world, throughout the centuries, who are either dabbling in the realm of the dead without understanding what they are doing, or are unaware of how their light is attracting the darker shadows of the underworld.

These hostile takeovers do not just occur with the uninitiated. They also happens with gifted practitioners whose profession includes calling on the dead for others in readings. I will share a true story about this later in the chapter that involves one of the most gifted necromancers I have ever met, and someone who was a very close and beloved friend of mine. For now, I want to shift into another type of non-physical spirit you must be aware of when bridging the world of the dead and living.

So far in this section, I have shared examples of spirits who were once human and show up with not-so-nice intentions once they have passed on. There is another group of spirits who are seeking to fulfill a different type of energetic exchange that are not by origin human. These are interdimensional entities lingering in the shadows between the seen and unseen world.

Rather than feeding off unhealthy addictions acquired as a living human, these entities seek out and consume the energy of human suffering. They are well equipped in applying manipulative and sinister intentions, having devised all sorts of ways to enter the world of form and wreak havoc on unsuspecting human beings.

These examples of the darker and more dangerous elements that can happen when dabbling in the underworld are not shared here to scare you from working with the dead and spirit realm. Instead, I am sharing to underscore the importance of calling on the dead with great respect and mindfulness. There are a variety of protective practices and measures you can employ to keep you and those you do readings for safe, some of which I will share later in the chapter.

Four Phases of Spirit Communication

With all practices of tea witchery, there are specific teas for every occasion and spirit communication is no different. There are teas that will aid in communicating with the dead. Specific tisanes of herbs, flowers, and trees will allow you to commune and understand the dead better when you drink the tea with them and acknowledge their presence.

To better understand how these teas work with spirit communication and how to properly apply them to assist in manifesting your intentions and desired outcomes, I have broken down the process of spirit communication into four distinct phases:

1. The transitioning
2. The connection
3. The vision
4. The voice

In the next section, I will share with you the different types of tea and incantation for each phase. Although the type of tea and incantation are both important, not to be overlooked is the way in which the tea is served.

When you are working with spirit communication and tea magic, you will want to offer the dead a cup of tea by placing it either on an altar or in a special location for them. As an offering to the dead or spirit realm, tea can be shared and enjoyed by drinking it with them. Tea and herbal blends can be offered as a gift to entice the dead back to the vibration of life.

Tea and Incantations

While the type of tea, and how you serve it, are the centerpiece of blending tea witchery with spirit communication, they are not the only important ingredients. By speaking an incantation to the spirit or the dead, this creates sound which establishes a vocal vibrational bridge for the spirit to follow to this side of the matrix. Keeping your intent clear in your incantation is important because the dead sometimes have limited focus, so it is up to you to guide them into giving you what you seek.

There are many ways to begin communicating with spirits, some of which we will get into further in this chapter. For this section, I want to share a poem I was guided to write, which I often speak out loud before engaging in tea magic rituals, especially if they involve spirit communication. The intention with this is to hold and create a light for the spirits to follow as they are transitioning from the world of the dead to the world of the living.

Tea Magic Poem (Incantation)

> *Brewing tea by candlelight.*
>
> *Infused with moonlight.*
>
> *Dazzled by starlight.*
>
> *Blessed by Divine light.*
>
> *Renewed in morning light.*
>
> *Charged with sunlight.*

I invite you to use this or make up one of your own. When you are writing an incantation or poem the words do not always have to rhyme, as you will see with some of those in the following four phases of spirit communication. They can also be specific to the ritual itself and the intentions, or a combination of the two. For me, this brief poem, which can be interpreted as an incantation, helps set the mood and the space energetically for a safe, protective, and blessed ritual with the spirit realm through tea magic.

Here, then, are the four phases of spirit communication and the corresponding tea and incantation.

The Transitioning

Tea: Lavender, thyme, and lemongrass tea will calm restless spirits to make communication easier. This tea helps to transition the newly dead to the other side and find peace.

Incantation

> *Lavender calms, eternal thyme, and lemongrass eases the restless mind.*
>
> *Tea as an offering for your place in time.*

The Connection

Tea: Parsley, marigold petals, wormwood, and bay leaf tea will aid in communication with the dead and spirits on the other side who have been undisturbed or dead for a long time.

Incantation

>   *Lush is parsley, life to hold.*
>
>   *Wormwood holding place of soul.*
>
>   *Bay leaf offering pays the toll.*
>
>   *Welcome back to warmth from cold.*

The Vision

Tea: Marigold flowers, mugwort, and apple tea will help bring the spirit into view so you can see them clearly both in your mind's eye, and in physical form of shadow, mist, or full apparition.

Incantation

>   *Marigold flowers for the eyes of the dead, bringing into sight the spirit that fled.*
>
>   *Herb of mugwort to open the eyes of mind, forming shape of the ties that bind.*
>
>   *Tangible the apple a gift for you, rise in form spirit true.*

The Voice

Tea: Cedar tips, wormwood, peppermint, and licorice root made into a tea will give voice to the spirit or dead to allow you to hear them clearly. This opens a clear channel of direct sounds, tones, and/or voice. This tea will also help prepare the medium's voice while the spirit takes possession and speaks through them.

Incantation

> *The winds that whisper through the cedar tips.*
>
> *Wormwood present for the lips.*
>
> *Peppermint leaf invigorates and stimulates, as the licorice root will lubricate.*
>
> *With this tea your voice is heard, bringing forth your spoken word.*

Protection and Precautions

When you are practicing spirit communication with tea magic, protecting yourself and those in the room with you is not something to take for granted. Mediums, necromancers, spirit board enthusiasts, and conjurers of the dead all understand how important it is to protect yourself from the unwanted lingering of the other side. Not all of them, however, remain consistent with protecting themselves.

You will come to see with the story of Ginger Marie, no matter how gifted you are or how long you have worked with the other side, that all it takes is one misstep and you can quickly find yourself on a slippery slope. For this reason, I chose to present this section, and the next three, before Ginger's story. This way you have proper context and appreciation for the importance of properly protecting yourself and all living things in the room when you are engaged in spirit communication and tea magic.

When working with spirits of the dead, especially those you are not familiar with, it is important to take precautions to protect yourself and those you are doing a reading for. Even if you are familiar with the spirit you are working with, it is quite possible for other darker or unwanted energy forces and spirits to sneak in when you are not looking. It is also common for practitioners to have grown too comfortable communicating with their preferred spirit and forget to properly prepare before each interaction.

The next three sections provide practical and proven practices for protection and precaution. The first introduces you to a powerful tea blend for protection that features tormentil root. The next section outlines some basic protection practices to use when calling in the dead. These two are followed by a brief section in which I share four types of stones that are ideal for safely guarding you from entities of darkness and unwanted attachments from the other side.

Tormentil Root

There is folk lore and old wives' tales about tormentil root protecting the living from the dead.[26] Whether it is used in a tea, a talisman, or mojo bag, or hung in your home it is effective in bringing protection to the living. The small yellow flowers will also bring joy and promote a happy home with everlasting love.

This root goes by many names. It is also known as bloodroot, earth bank, biscuits, five finger grass, thorn mantle, shepherds knot, English sarsaparilla, and red root and has also been called flesh and blood.

Tormentil root made into a tea will help protect you from permanent possession. This is especially helpful for mediums and those participating in seances or other forms of conjuring the dead. This root will also make sure you do not bring any undead, restless, dark, or sly trickster spirits back with you when you are traveling between worlds. This root lends strength to your life force, so you make it back safely and unharmed.

To aid in the healing of any flesh wounds begot on the other side or that the spirit or dead may have inflicted while on the side of the living, you can do the following. Blend together equal parts of tormentil root, calendula, and rose. When these herbs are made into a poultice and placed in clean white cotton, they can be applied to the wound to speed up the healing process. This blend can also seal the wound so the entity cannot re-enter the body, take possession, or continue to harm the living.

Another effective blend with tormentil root includes brewing it with chamomile, rose, and green tea. Drink this tea to soothe the body and release any fatigue and pressure the entity may have left behind. Made into a tea bath, this blend will wash away any ectoplasmic residue and dissolve any cords that may have been attached by the entity or any interdimensional hitchhikers you may have picked up while you were interacting in the other world.

---

26. Illes, *The Element Encyclopedia of 5,000 Spells.*

The mixture of tormentil root, chamomile, rose, and green tea can also be used to wipe down Ouija boards, tarot cards, or any other divination tools used as a porthole or bridge to the shadowlands. This will neutralize and stop your tools from allowing any more entries to the side of the living.

If you are an astral traveler or astral projector, I also recommend you drink a cup of this tea before projecting. Doing so beforehand can protect your physical body and your etheric body while you are astral projecting your spirit body into the astral realm. Even if you drink this tea blend before, it is always good to drink the tea and use it as tea wash afterward. Sometimes hitchhiking spirits, entities, and sly sneaky vibrations can attach themselves to you while you are in the astral dimension. If you feel you have brought something back with you when you were on a journey, use the tea and tea bath to release and dissolve it.

Spirit Protection Practices

In this section, I am going to share with you a variety of basic protection practices to consider applying when calling in the dead.

When calling in spirits for the first time, it is advisable to call in one you may already know, such as a relative you met while they were living. You can also call on a relative whom you are related to that you did not meet. These spirits are mostly harmless and want to communicate with you, making it a safe and, potentially, a profoundly positive experience.

If you are scared about doing this, or someone with you carries fears about connecting with the other side, even if you are trying to contact a loved one, I would not recommend you attempt doing so for the following reasons. Fear attracts malevolent spirits, as they feed off fear. When you or someone else is in a state of fear, this can weaken your energy field, giving malevolent spirits additional strength. To be in a lower vibrational state, which is what fear is, makes it easier for these types of spirits to attach themselves to you or another, and from there, they deplete you of joy and light. So, take heed, and put yourself in a state of joy leading up to and during the practice of spirit communication and tea magic. One easy way to do this is to reminisce about happy times with the spirit you are calling. This type of light will add a protection layer around you and others in the room, including your ancestor, shielding out any unwanted negative spirits.

Precautions to Take Before Calling in the Dead

State clearly who you are calling. State that you are seeking benevolent spirits who mean no harm or negativity. Upon finishing your reading, immediately sage or use a room-clearing spray for the room you did your reading in to release any remaining vibration or spirit residue. For example, you could say, "I call upon my ancestors to share with me this cup of tea in love, light, and protection, to bring in wisdom and guidance. You are welcomed in this space."

Another example could be, "All negative forces that cause harm, bring illness, and lurk in negativity are banished from this room. You are not welcomed here."

Creating a sacred and protected space by casting a circle and calling in directions, corners, guardian(s), or Archangels also works well for protection and aids in creating a clear and illuminated space for facilitating your readings, or channelings. There are two excellent books by Jason Mankey to check out: *Transformative Witchcraft* and *Witches Wheel of the Year*. These books give in-depth examples of what is involved in creating circles of protection.

Cleaning Your Reading Area

It is most helpful to sage your reading area after you have channeled spirits. If smoke is an issue, you can create a spray. Here is one I use for my own readings when sage is not available.

Room-Clearing Spray

Mix up in a spray bottle and shake before each use:

- 12 to 16 ounces of lightly steeped green tea, cooled
- 9 drops of white sage essential oil
- A pinch of sea salt
- Add a jet stone to the bottom of bottle

You can embellish and personalize your spray by adding additional essential oils that resonate best with you and are in alignment with the kind of readings or channelings that you are doing. Oils such as rose, wild orange, or peppermint tea are always good choices.

When using your spray, same as it is with using sage, it is always a good idea to express gratitude out loud for the spirits that have stepped in to answer questions. After thanking them, kindly ask that they return to where they came from. If you feel that something heavier has stepped in, be sterner in your demand, reinforce this by telling them they are not welcomed here, and state "leave now."

Stones for Spirit Communication

Stones are not only great for charging your tea, but particular stones can also safely guard you from entities of darkness and unwanted attachments from the other side. In this case, there are four that myself and others have found to be consistently effective.

Storing these stones in your tea cupboard or apothecary will keep your teas and herbs energetically protected from outside influences. You might consider them in jewelry, or pieces of them in the corners of the room you are working in or on the table you are working on.

Here are the four ideal stones for safely guarding you, and those you are doing a reading with, from entities of darkness and unwanted attachments from the other side.

Jet Stone

A black stone that is light in weight called jet is used to draw out negativity and alleviate fears. It is used for protection on spiritual journeys to keep away entities of darkness.

Peridot

This stone has been used to protect the aura by keeping away evil spirits. Peridot sharpens your mind and opens new levels of awareness, helping you to connect with your higher spirit and spirit guides.

Smoky Quartz

This stone helps to keep your energy grounded and centered. This stone has a strong connection with the earth and can neutralize electromagnetic and unwanted other worldly vibrations.

Clear Quartz

One of the most important of the quartz family, this stone is used for protection and amplification of focus. This stone is a powerful ally when used in conjunction with other stones to create a stronger charge and enhanced energy.

Tea Parties with the Dead

For those who are new to tea parties with the dead, you may be surprised there is such a thing. More than a current trend, tea parties with the dead are an ancient tradition, and fill an important and enjoyable role in tea witchery. In this chapter, I am going to share with you the best time to have a tea party with the dead, what to say to open the space, proper clothing if it is a tea party for a recently deceased relative or friend, and best practices for honoring the dead at a tea party.

Opening the Space

Opening the space is a time-honored tradition with any magical practice, especially when you are going to have tea with your ancestors who are now part of the spirit world. There are many ways to open the space, some of which I have shared in previous chapters. One of the most effective is speak your intentions out loud, which can also be woven into an invocation.

When you are going to have tea with one or more of your ancestors, it is always a good thing to speak their names or titles in the family out loud and clearly state your intentions, both for you and for them. If you have specific questions or a desire to know something, be sure to share this as well.

Here then is a place to start, with a basic introduction and method for speaking your intentions to your ancestors:

To my mother, her mother, my great-grandmother, and the mothers
that have come before.

I invite you in to share a pot of tea with me.

Share with me your wisdom of decades past.

Enjoy with me a cup of tea from a century away.

Allow me to tell you about the week I have been having.

A cup of tea solves everything.

Laugh with me as I blunder through it.

Share with me how you did it.

Because I am here, sharing a cup of tea ...

... with my mothers and ancestors who have walked before me.

As is the case with all the invocations, incantations, and intentions I have provided you with examples of, please follow your own inner guidance as to whether you want to include your own distinct version or create a hybrid of the ones in the book and your own.

A Good Time for Tea

Enjoying tea with your ancestors can happen anytime. For me, and many people I know, anytime is always teatime. This applies to enjoying tea with your ancestors. Although tea with your ancestors can happen at any time, when it does happen, an important role for you to assume is that of a genuinely attentive listener.

I believe that if you listen, your ancestors have the best advice. You are the breath of their breath, blood of their blood, and you can feel them resonate in your bones. You know when they are there. I often hear my grandmothers laugh in my ear, a familiar moment I cannot explain, a memory that flashes by and puts a big smile on my face.

One of the reasons their advice is always spot on is because they have walked this earth before you and have a keen awareness of you that many other people, living or dead, do not have. Ancestors paved the way for the path you are currently on. You are created from thousands of years of their love. And for most ancestors, they would love nothing more than to witness you shine your light at this moment in your journey.

I often refer to my teatime with ancestors as a form of tea meditation. Although you are speaking out loud, to hear and feel into what your ancestors are saying requires you to ease into a meditative-like state. This way, your mind chatter subsides, and you are clearing space in your mind to receive the wisdom, advice, and reflections your ancestors will share.

Tea meditation can encompass a brief visit with their memory or can be something deeper and a little more intimate as you might focus on a question or seek deeper advice. Sharing tea can be as simple as making an extra cup and placing it on the table across from you, placing a cup of tea on an altar in your relative's name, or simply thinking about them while you drink your cup of tea.

This kind of tea meditation with your ancestor can happen at any time or any place the notion strikes you. Nothing fancy, just a moment in time and a cup of tea.

Tea Party Honoring the Dead

Whereas tea meditation with your ancestors requires little preparation and can occur pretty much anywhere at any time, that is not the case with creating a tea party with the dead. Tea parties for your ancestors can be a lovely holiday celebration or can take place on special days. I suggest this tea party ritual should take place when the veils between the realms are thinnest. This would be sometime during the week of October 27 to November 3.

That week lines itself up with the Día de los Muertos celebrations in Mexico, the European All Saints Day, and Pagan Samhain, which morphed the holiday known as Halloween. All these holidays are associated with the dead and the shadow side, and each of them is celebratory in nature.

Because of the timing, a tea party honoring the dead during this time of year gives you plenty of opportunities to properly prepare. In the next section, I am going to share with you how to prepare and set up such a party.

Arranging a Tea Party for the Dead

As with any party, there will be guests, a theme, and the necessary items to make sure your guests will enjoy themselves and your overall intentions for the party are fulfilled. With that in mind, here are the basics for what you will need to arrange a tea party for the dead. You will need a small group of guests (between three and seven people), a photograph or object related each ancestor invited to tea, a teacup for each guest and a teacup for each ancestor, a tea light for each guest, tea and teapots sufficient for the number of guests, small sweet treats or traditional tea cakes, and a pot of marigold flowers.

Invite your family or close friends of the family to this tea. Ask your guests to bring a photograph or object special to a relative they would like to connect with and honor. Invite age-appropriate youth who may not have met their ancestors, as this will be a wonderful introduction to them.

The reason I suggest keeping the guest list between three to seven people, is that it allows for an intimate gathering and affords everyone a chance to engage with their ancestors. Be sure to have enough teacups for each guest and each ancestor. If each family member brings a different ancestor, there will be a maximum of fourteen cups of tea on your table. If two or more guests bring the same ancestor, they can share the same ancestor's teacup.

Think about where you are having this tea party and the space you're having it in. Choose a table to seat all your guests. The dining room should be fine if you have one. The center of the table is where your guests will place the photograph of their ancestor, so make sure there is room for a cup of tea in front of the picture. A few candles and flower petals around them are a nice touch.

Decorations should be a mix of flowers and candles, not just on the table but in the home and space where your guests will mingle. Also, be sure to ask your guests to bring additional photographs and special items of the ancestor. These can both be placed on the main table, but with the possibility of limited space on the table, you may want to prepare other designated spaces for these items. If you have your grandmother's china set or teacups, this would be a perfect place to use them in honor of her.

Place small sweets and traditional tea cakes among the photographs and around the table. If you have your great-grandmother's cookie or candy recipe, be sure to make those and bring them. Again, based on the space and size of main dining table, it may be a good thing to have another table or two, possibly card tables draped with nice linen as backups. This way, the sweets and tea cakes can be easy to get to. The last thing you want is for your guests to unintentionally knock anything on the dining table over when trying to reach a scone, cookie, or other sweet treat.

Ceremony with the Dead

When all guests are seated and the objects related to the ancestors are placed in the center of the table, the host welcomes the guests and their ancestors to tea. Tea service begins, and everyone pours a cup of tea for themselves.

The host begins by providing a summary of the proceedings. The host lets their guests know they will initiate the proceedings with their ancestor. Following that, each guest is invited to introduce their ancestor and to share a brief story about them. Be sure to let your guests know that sharing openly is not obligatory; if they wish to honor their ancestor silently, that is perfectly acceptable.

From there, the host introduces their ancestor and explains to everyone how they are related. The host then tells a brief story about their ancestor and shares a memory they have of them.

"I have invited our great-Aunt Minnie." As you say their name, acknowledge the photograph of the relative in the center of the table. At this time, light the tea light, and set it in front of the photo or object. After doing this, pour a cup of tea for your ancestor and place it next to the photo and candle.

Address your ancestor as if they were there. Here is an example:

"Aunt Minnie, it is lovely to have you here with us. We are all honored by your presence. I remember you could whistle any tune and hit every note. The family would say you could whistle like a bird. Thank you for teaching me how to whistle. I still whistle to this day, and it brings me great joy knowing you were the one who showed me how. Welcome to the tea party."

Next, the host asks that if anyone else has a story about Aunt Minnie, this is their opportunity to share. It is important to note that if the guest is joined by other family members, and they have a connection to Aunt Minnie, it is customary to allow space for them to share as well. When guests are done relating their experience with Aunt Minnie, or if no one else has a story to share, the host will indicate it is now time for the next guest to introduce their relative.

The next guest will either remain sitting or stand as they introduce their relative and shares how they are related. Like the host did, the guest lights the tea light candle and pours their ancestor a cup of tea. The guest will then proceed to share a memory or story of the ancestor and concludes by welcoming them to the tea party.

This process should continue around the table until each ancestor has had their candle lit and their tea poured, and has been remembered. When the circle of introductions and stories have come to completion, conclude the tea with your ancestors by saying the following:

Host says, "Stay if you will, leave if you must, thank you for having tea with us."

While each ancestor is being remembered, it is acceptable to enjoy your tea and treats as you listen to their memory and stories.

Tips for Tea with the Dead

By this point, you may be more excited than ever to commune with the dead through a tea party in their honor. Yet, due to where you live, and the number of people in your life who may or may not be open to such a gathering, a tea party to honor your ancestors and the ancestors of others might not be practical at this time. Tea with your ancestors can be modified to only one ancestor if you wish, and it could just involve you and your chosen ancestor. This could be a tea party of remembrance or a tea party to say goodbye.

If it is a tea party celebrating or honoring one relative, whether it is just you or another person, everything we have covered applies.

If this is a tea party to say goodbye to a recently crossed-over relative, as a show of respect for the dead, add a black tablecloth to your table where this tea will be held. You might also want to wear black and advise your guest or guests to also wear black. A tea gathering for the recent dead is to honor the memory of their spirit. It is a time to say your last goodbyes if you weren't able to make it to the funeral service or meet with them before they crossed over.

As with many of the tea witchery practices, I advise you to have your tea party anyway you like it. It is your party, after all, and it is your ancestors or recently passed relatives or friends that you are honoring. You know them best. In whatever ways you choose to prepare and throw a tea party for the deceased, always keep in mind what your ancestors would like, and you would like.

Now, if you are calling on ancestors you never met, or wonder if they liked tea, I guarantee that your ancestors drank tea somewhere in time. So, when you get that inner calling that you would like to engage with them, or you feel their presence, fix them a cup of tea, and tell them about your day. But this is not just about you talking. Listen to their advice and pay attention to the signs around you if you ask them for help.

The Story of Ginger Marie

Now that you have a good frame of reference for why and how to protect yourself and those you do spirit communication readings with, or those you engage with in tea parties with the dead, I want to conclude this chapter with the true story of Ginger Marie. It is my intention that no matter what your experience is in working with the dead, and whether tea magic is involved or not, this story serves as a lifelong reminder of what can happen when you stop protecting yourself and your environment during and after spirit communication readings.

I met Ginger Marie at a psychic fair in Dallas, Texas, many years ago. She was the most gifted psychic and medium I have ever met. Her gift for communicating with the other side was unlike anything I have ever experienced before or since. After being friends for a couple years, I invited Ginger to come to work at my aromatherapy and metaphysical shop Body of Sun.

One day she came into the shop and sat down, business as usual. I noticed she slipped into her trance-like state, but there was no one there except the two of us. She then said to me, "Sissy, the ring is behind the dresser."

"Wait? What?" I spoke, rather shocked that she not only spoke these words but used "Sissy." Saying "Sissy" was a bolt to my heart, for that is what my grandmother used to call me when I was a child.

Without any pause between the trance state and what she just said, Ginger sprang back into conscious state, looked at me with a glassy-eyed stare, and said,

"Someone wants you to know that." What she did not know is that earlier in the day, before leaving for the shop, I was looking for my grandmother's ring. I had not been able to find it for months, and I was convinced someone stole it.

Later that night, following the guidance that came through Ginger, I found the ring. It was behind the dresser, wedged in between where the mirror was attached to the base of the drawers. Overwhelmed with immense gratitude and joy, I sat there for several minutes crying, holding the ring in my hand. I knew Ginger was gifted but I had no idea the ease and seamless flow she had with allowing the other side to communicate through her, when and where it was needed most.

In the shop we would sometimes jokingly and lovingly call Ginger "the Saint" because her clients would come in completely distraught, only to leave with a peaceful calmness about them. They would rave and sing Ginger's praise, each of them a living testimonial to her ability to ease their worries about their loved one on the other side.

I once asked Ginger about her gift, wondering if she could provide additional insight into how she does what she does. She said it was easy for her, like second nature. She added that she still needed to learn the ins and outs of interacting with the spirit realm. The part that was hardest for her was when the dead share with her how they died. She said that is usually the first thing they want to impart to her, which she said was not all they imparted.

When explaining how they died, sometimes these spirits would leave a piece of the pain inside Ginger that she would have to release later. For example, if they died of a heart attack, she would feel pain in her heart. Any kind of a physical accident that befell them, that too would be temporarily imprinted on Ginger, usually through a sharp burst of pain in her body.

Ginger was the one who told me about using blood root and tormentil to keep herself protected from the other side. Her preferred method of use was to bathe in it. She said it would take the pain away. She would also make a spray that she would add the essential oil of white sage to, and a piece of jet stone in the bottle. She would spray this in the reader room after every reading. She would sometimes make tea out of tormentil root, which usually was due to difficulty shaking off the spirit or if the spirit was staying too long. Drinking the tea would close her connection to the other side.

Closing the other side from accessing her and communicating was essential to a balanced life. Although Ginger made her living by bringing spirits through, there was no way she could live any semblance of a quality life keeping herself open twenty-four hours a day.

Ginger really was a saint and I learned a great deal from her. During most of our friendship, Ginger would teach me her methods of protection from the other side. She once remarked, that if she were not so meticulous and diligent with these protective measures, not only would her work suffer, but she would not have made it this far. This always stuck with me and remains to this day, one of the reasons my attention to protective measures is so acute and unwavering. Unfortunately, Ginger's attention to these details eventually waned and the results were not good.

A Dark Entity Arrives

I do not know when, but at some point Ginger stopped using the spray and fixing the tormentil root tea and drinking it after she did readings at the store. I never asked her why or even inquired if she was regularly protecting herself as she had been for so many years prior. I do know, however, that it was around the same time Ginger started becoming sicker.

It went beyond just physical illness, as Ginger's emotional and mental state began to deteriorate. Her bubbly and inviting demeanor faded, as she began doing and saying things that would just baffle me and the spiritual and witch communities we were in. To Ginger's credit she stopped doing readings for some time to get a handle on what was happening. Unfortunately, the darkness never left.

Not long after moving to California, a mutual friend from Texas rang me up to inform me Ginger had laid her body down on the railroad tracks, ending her life. To release herself from the clutches of this entity or entities that were driving her mad, for Ginger, this was her only way out.

I am not going to lie and say the news of Ginger's death did not hit me hard, because it did. Rather than remember her for how she was in her final year or two of life, I see her for who she truly was: a saint and a beacon of light, so bright, that not only did living souls get drawn to her, but so did the dead. She will always be remembered by me as a friend, and even a mentor in many magical practices, not the least of which is what to do and not do when communicating with the spiritual world.

Next Steps with Spirit Communication

For those of you just now being introduced to spirit communication, after reading the story of Ginger Marie, I can understand you may be hesitant to engage in spirit communication, let alone have a tea party with the dead. It is not the dead we should fear but our lack of respect for the spirit realm, and with it, a lack of preparation and protection.

It is because of Ginger that I have learned all the names of tormentil and how to use it. Because of her, I highly suggest that mediums of all levels take great care in their protection rituals and equally important, to take long breaks from allowing spirits to come through. I understand your income is based on how many readings you give, but as Ginger clearly showed, when you are overworked, your physical and mental health become compromised, leaving you highly vulnerable to attacks and unwanted entities.

For newbies who are just beginning to exercise your gifts of exploring new paths in spirit communication and tea magic, please take heed and listen to the advice of others. Learn from their experiences and take time to develop and strengthen your knowledge before traveling too deep and too far into the underworld.

And finally, before enjoying tea with the dead, in whatever way you feel comfortable, I highly encourage you to follow the precautionary measures and protective practices outlined in this chapter. Although you do not want to enter the space of enjoying a cup of tea with your ancestor or to put together a tea party for the dead with a sense of dread, it is always advisable to prepare the space where the dead are called in and protect all living things in that space.

Acknowledging your ancestors or a family member who has crossed over with a cup of tea is a way of keeping their memory alive and their love strong in your heart. Tea can act as the tie that binds to keep them near and dear to you and your family.

There are an endless number of ways to commune with the dead that includes tea. Here are some reminders and best practices.

When working with the other realm, try mixing your own brew with the herbs I referenced in the chapter along with your other favorite herbs, teas, and roots. Doing so will aid in your specific spirit communication, clairvoyance, and summonsing.

There are also a variety of ways to include gemstones in your spirit communication work before, during, and after the readings. Among practitioners of gemstone healing, the picture jasper is a powerful grounding stone that promotes connection to the earth. Some view this stone as a direct message from Earth itself, instilling a sense of proportion, bringing comfort, alleviating fear, and cultivating harmony.

Adding a piece of the picture jasper to the teapot that you are brewing tea in will facilitate smooth communications with the other side, keeping the spirit or entity focused on the message it is bringing. Picture jasper also helps to make the message clear and understandable.

Whatever you choose as your next steps with tea magic and spirit communication, remember to always protect yourself, your location, and any other living things in the room with you, even if it is a simple incantation or protection circle.

When done through a state of conscious awareness and proper protection, and infused with genuinely loving intentions and joyous energy, spirit communication is not only safe, but it is a whole lot of fun! Most of all, bring with you into all communication with the dead a genuine respect, an abundance of happiness, and a good cup of tea.

Chapter 11

Tea Rituals and Moon Magic

Through her ever-present and ever-changing cycle, the omnipresent nature of the moon is showering Earth, and all life on it, with auspicious and powerful energies. Even when the moon is not visible, she is directly affecting our lives on many levels, both the seen and unseen. More than just a celestial body, the moon reflects our inner emotions. When you have taken the time to understand the correspondences and archetypal nature of the moon's eight primary cycles, you will come to know your inner self on a much deeper, and far more intimate scale.

Like most kitchen witches, or anyone who dabbles in magic, your magical practices will invariably come into alignment with one or more of the moon's cycles. Since the moon's cycles are intimately tied into all our emotional states of mind, and to the divine feminine cycle, your magic may start out as a rather unconscious interaction with the moon's energies. The more you open yourself to the nature of the moon's energies, the more conscious and intentional you are with what magical practices to engage in, what intentions to set, and what tea to drink during specific times of the month.

As I have pointed out in earlier chapters, many of the topics and themes I have framed around tea magic serve as an introduction to their origins and fundamental essence. That is certainly the case here with tea rituals to use with moon magic. Therefore, this chapter is not a full-spectrum analysis on the moon, nor is it an in-depth look into the myriad ways you can consciously work with her frequencies and energy. Instead, what you will discover in this chapter is designed to expand your awareness of magical moon practices with specific tea rituals so you can more confidently choose which form of moon magic to pair with your favorite blends of tea.

The Sun and the Moon

To better understand and fully appreciate the cycles of the moon, it is important to first know how the moon is represented in human behavior. That also means knowing the relationship the moon has to the sun.

The sun and the moon have been worshiped, in some capacity, by most ancient cultures, as they recognized these two planets directly affect our thoughts, emotions, and behaviors. These cultures created their own distinct rituals, based on the understanding and metaphorical interpretation of the sun and moon. Therefore, the saying "as above, so below" can be clearly seen when we look at how the sun and moon represent our inner and outer selves here on Earth, for without these two planets, life as we know it would not exist.

The sun metaphorically represents our masculine archetype, and thus, the outer structure of the world, from our personality and identity to the way we physically show up in the world. Whereas, the moon represents our feminine archetype, and thus, the inner workings of our inner world, such as the emotions and desires we keep hidden, either knowingly or unknowingly. That is why the moon is most associated with shadow work, where we enter the unknown, to uncover and unlock the secrets of who we truly are.

From an astrological perspective, where the sun is in terms of the zodiac determines the energy, viewability, and timing of a new moon and full moon, and everything in between these cycles. For instance, when there is a new moon, the moon and sun are in the same zodiac sign and are at the same degree in that sign. For this reason and more, during a new moon the energy required for birthing new things in life, such as focus and creativity, are enhanced during a new moon cycle.

When the moon is in her full moon cycle, the sun is sitting opposite of the moon. This is when the full moon is illuminated in all her glorious nature. It can only happen when the sun and the moon are at the same degree, but in opposite zodiac signs. Because the sun and moon are opposing one another at this time of each month, from an energetic perspective, full moons have been known for centuries to stir up people's emotions in some uncomfortable ways. That does not mean your inner werewolf is unleashed. It does mean that the full moon also represents an auspicious time to get your inner feminine and inner masculine energies in harmonic alignment, mentally, spiritually, and magically.

Cycles of the Moon

There are eight cycles of the moon, and they can be broken down into four main areas: new moon, waxing moon, full moon, waning moon. Here are the full eight cycles, in the order in which they unfold:

1. New moon
2. Waxing crescent moon
3. First quarter moon
4. Waxing gibbous moon
5. Full moon
6. Waning gibbous moon
7. Last quarter moon
8. Waning crescent moon

For this section, I am going to share some brief, fundamental insights on the four primary cycles, beginning with the new moon.

New Moon

The new moon represents the beginning of the month, and thus, a new moon cycle. For this reason, a new moon has been identified as the ideal energy to set new intentions and goals, and to initiate new beginnings.

When there is a new moon that means the sun and moon are in the same zodiac sign. It is also when the moon is least visible, and that is because it is between the sun and the earth. For this reason, the side of the moon that we see from Earth is not viewable due to where the sun's rays are shining on it. The term *dark side of the moon* is not just a famous album from the iconic rock band Pink Floyd; it relates to where the sun is shining during a new moon.

Waxing Moon

If the new moon is an ideal opportunity for new ideas and new beginnings, the next cycle of the moon, which is waxing moon, is represented by the momentum of your desires growing. This is represented during the waxing moon as you can visually see slivers of the moon beginning to come into view. It is also a period of the month, where unconscious fears and programs running in the shadows can sprout up and derail your best efforts. For this reason, the waxing moon energies are a good time to get grounded and begin releasing anything that is no longer serving your highest and best interests.

Full Moon

In terms of the calendar cycle, when the full moon lights up our night sky, it is either at the mid-point or near the end of a given month. As I shared earlier, it is also when the sun and the moon are on direct opposite sides of the zodiac. Going back to the energetic essence of the new moon, where the seeds of new ideas and new beginnings are planted, the full moon represents when they come into full view.

This means your desires are amplified, which is why a tea ritual during the full moon is ideal for getting clear on what you truly desire to manifest into your new reality. If your desires are amplified, so too can your inner fears be illuminated. For this reason, the dichotomy of a full moon's energy can bring your personal vibration to full strength and controlled power over your body, mind, spirit, and magic.

If you are experiencing emotional and spiritual insecurities during a full moon, these vibrations too will become enhanced and shine bright in the mirror of the full moon. This allows you to see where you are needing to seek balance and truth, and to gain additional clarity on what to release that no longer serves you.

Waning Moon

During the waning moon cycle, the reverse of what occurs from the new moon to the full moon takes place. This means that during the three days or so that the full moon was illuminated by the sun, now the light is decreasing, hence the term waning. Energetically speaking, this is the time of the month for introspection.

By this point in the moon cycle, you would have seen what is working and not working in your life, at least in terms of the new ideas and new beginnings you gave birth to at the start of the moon's current cycle. If the new moon is seen as a cosmic reset, which many people refer to it as, this makes the waning moon an ideal time for reviewing your inner and outer journey in the previous weeks of the month, or even previous months and years of your life.

For these reasons, the waning moon cycle is an ideal time to celebrate your growth. Even if you still feel there is a ways to go with a specific idea or desire fully manifesting, you can observe your process and progress in a particular month or go bigger and see it from a vantage point of many years of unfoldment. In whatever ways you choose to observe your journey, be sure to always do so with an open mind and a grateful heart.

Charging Tea Water with the Moon Cycles

If you would like to charge your tea water to any of the moon cycles, all you need to do is place it under that moon. If you have bought water by the gallon from a supermarket or a water station, put it in the container you wish to store it in. When the moon is out, it is best to place the water outside so the rays of the moon can shine down on it and bathe the water in its silvery light. You can also place your tea water in a windowsill to catch the light.

You can charge the tea water for as long or as often as you like. You should, however, remove the water before daybreak. If you are working with a three-day charge, be sure to cover the water each day during daylight hours. Only uncover at night when you place it back in its charging place.

If it is cloudy, that is okay, as the moon is still there, and her energy is still just as potent. If you cannot open the window that you have placed your water in front of, again, that will not affect the moon's energy, as it will still reach through the window and properly charge your water.

This method of charging your tea water with the moon will work for all the phases of the moon and water infusion, be it the full moon, new moon, waxing moon, waning moon, blue moon, or black moon.

As you place your tea water beneath the moon of your choosing, it is traditional to ask the moon for help in energizing it. You can do this by a simple prayer or acknowledgment, or perhaps you have written special instructions for the moon. All are welcome. In general, a genuine please and a thank you will go a long way, whether you dress it up in an elaborate spell or incantation, or you simply say please and thank you. Manners always matter in tea magic and tea making.

This method of charging also applies to working with the moon's energy in conjunction with larger bodies of water as well. You can take your jugs of water right down to the lake, river, or stream and secure them in a spot in the water under the moon. Again, be sure to use manners when asking for the power of the body of water to recharge and activate the water you are placing in its care.

For example, if you are placing a jug of water in a lake you might say something like, "Moon … or Lake _____ (if the lake has a name, use it), I thank you for infusing your calm and soothing vibration into this jug of water. Thank you for your deep internal wisdom and meditative energy you share with this water. I accept and receive your aid with gratitude and love."

When giving gratitude, do not get too caught up in formalities; graces that come from the heart are the most enduring and true.

If you are camping, or you have time to brew a cup of tea you might want to make the moon and lake a cup of tea and pour it in slowly as an offering of gratitude for the moon and for the serenity the body of water has given you for your teas and potion making. I suggest you do this whether you are charging in a lake, stream, river, or waterfall.

Full Moon Tea Ritual

Full moon tea magic is designed to call forth the things you seek. This is also why full moon energy is supportive of releasing what you no longer need. For if you are going to call in what you want in your life, you will need to make room for it.

The full moon tea ritual I am sharing with you here can be applied for both a solo ceremony and small group participation.

This is an intensely personal tea ceremony between you and a significant cycle of the moon. Though it was first written as a solo tea and moon cycle meditation, I have since performed it in small, trusted groups and moon covens. This is a twenty-eight-day ritual and takes dedication, so be sure the friends you are working with can commit when deciding if you will do this solo or in a group.

One of the benefits of working in a group is that your power of manifestation will be greater if you are all focusing on the same outcome. For example, the group may call forth a change in the community, for harmony among friends and family, or to call forth money to open a joint venture or business together. Here is what you will need:

+ Charged moon water—2 gallons (if working in a group each person will need 2 gallons of water)—There are 32 cups of water between 2 gallons. If you are using larger cups for your tea, keep in mind you will need more water.
+ Teacup
+ Teapot
+ 1 white candle
+ 1 black candle or dark purple candle
+ 1 white piece of paper

If you are seeking clarity during your full moon ritual, choose a tea with gingko biloba, lavender, rosemary, or white tea to enhance clear thinking. If you are seeking prosperity, choose a mint-based or licorice and cinnamon tea. If you are seeking health, choose a green tea. If you are seeking love, choose a tea or herbal combination containing roses.

Perhaps blend your own personal brew containing the proper herbs, flowers, and teas for drawing in what it is you are manifesting or meditating on.

Full moon cycles last three days.

On the first day of the full moon, gather your all your supplies and lay them out beneath the beauty and potency of the moon's illuminated presence. If placing your items outside is not feasible, you can choose to set them up in a room where the moon shines through.

First Day of the Full Moon

Once you have what you need, it is now time to focus on your intention. I invite you to enter into a dialogue with the moon, by asking for its assistance.

Here is an example you can use, or rewrite for your own unique expression:

> I (or we) come to you, Silver Moon, to ask you to bestow your silver light and guiding energy onto these objects. To aid in the clarity of water, to enhance the power of the tea, to give a brightness to the candle, to consecrate the teacup and teapot as charged vessels to hold your illuminating and blessed guiding light in.

After your ritual tools have been charged for no less than one hour, or left out longer, pack them up and keep them away from the light to be used on the next night. I do not recommend you leave your ritual tools out until the morning, where the sun's rays will hit them.

Second Day of the Full Moon

On the second day of the full moon, this is when it is at its fullest.

Dress for your tea ritual, ideally choosing anything in white, silver, creams, or light greys. Anything that makes you feel magical and powerful.

Be respectful to the full moon and be respectful to yourself. Your clothing represents the moon's reflection in you. Therefore, silver jewelry and moonstones are perfect accessories to reflect the full moon's light.

Place your white candle, teacup, and paper on a clear clean table, outside and under the moonlight or in a room where the full moon shines through a window.

Use the water from the gallon you charged the night before to brew your teapot.

Sit down with your pot of tea and pour yourself a cup. If you are working with a group, be sure to make enough tea for everyone. Light the candle. Title and date your paper that you will write on. You can use what you are seeking as a title, or you can simply write somethings basic such as: *Full Moon Tea Ritual* and the date.

With clear intentions and focus, handwrite and ask the full moon to help you find the things you are seeking by shining her illuminating light on them and the path for you to reach them.

Drink your tea and imbue the essence of her silvery light. Do not rush yourself. Take your time and be clear in your desires.

Allow the full moon to shine on your written words. Fold up the paper and place on the windowsill under the moonlight or on your altar. This is not to be opened again.

If being done in a group, everyone participating must contribute to this paper by handwriting what it is the group is seeking. Another option is that each person can write a different thing as long as all things have been decided on by the whole of the group prior to this point in the ritual.

The paper must be assigned to one person's altar and not be opened. After this, it is time to chant over your teacup and drink the tea. Here is a chant you can use to further amplify your ritual on the second night of the full moon:

Calling forth the things I (we) seek by candlelight.

I (we) share this tea under the full moon at night.

Receptive to clear answers, thankful for clear sight.

When you are ready, pour a cup of tea for the full moon and leave it in her light, either outside, on a windowsill, or on an altar if there is no direct light from the moon.

Third Day of the Full Moon

On the third night of the full moon, whether you are working solo or in a group, everyone will be at their own locations for this part of the ritual.

Make two cups of tea using the charged water and tea or tea blend that was charged under the full moon two days prior. One cup for yourself, and one for the full moon. Light a white candle.

Hold clearly in your mind the intent of this meditation and tea with the full moon, the paper you have written on, and the connection between moonlight and candlelight, as both are guides in the night and illumination.

Here is a chant you can use to further amplify your ritual on the third and final night of the full moon:

> *Calling forth the things I (we) seek by candlelight.*
>
> *I (we) share this tea under the full moon at night.*
>
> *Receptive to clear answers, thankful for clear sight.*

For the next thirteen days, in the leadup to the new moon, you should have a cup of tea every night that is brewed with your charged full moon water. Recall what it is that you sent the full moon to seek on your behalf and illuminate for you. As the full moon wanes and fades, know that she is retrieving your requests. During these thirteen days, it is not necessary to make the moon a cup of tea, unless you feel guided to.

New Moon Tea Ritual

The new moon is the halfway point to this tea magic and moon meditation and is the next part of interactive participation.

The new moon is upon you. Thirteen days has passed since the full moon, and your unwavering dedication to your nightly tea with the moon has now come to darkness. There is no moon in the night. The moon has gone deep into the other side to bring back the things you asked of her. It is now time to prepare the three-day ritual ceremony with the new moon.

To prepare for tea with the new moon, wear darker-color clothes such as black, purple, or dark grey. This is to reflect the distance between you and the new moon, while also honoring the darker, more personal side of the moon. Jewelry such as dark stones of onyx, hematite, and sapphires are ideal. Brew your pot of tea with your full moon charged water and tea. Prepare one cup for you, and one cup for the new moon. If you are performing this ritual with a group, make enough tea for everyone, and one cup for the new moon is plenty. On this night, know that the new moon begins her journey home to you, bringing with her the things you have asked for. The dark time of the sky, therefore, is a time of introspection and a time to go inside yourself and seek personal truths and answers.

As you drink your tea and recall the things you requested of the full moon, ask yourself if you did all you could do to help the moon in its delivery. What could you have done to help facilitate what you have asked for? Note in your mind what you will do to help manifest these requests into your life.

Light your purple or black candle. Whisper your name into the flame of the candle. Allow the candle to serve as a guiding light for the new moon on this night. Place the candle in a windowsill or outside under the sky. Your altar will work if you cannot get direct sky contact. If you are working in a group for this new moon ritual, use one candle for the first day of the new moon. Each person should whisper their name into the flame, or the name of what it is they are seeking.

Drink your tea and recommit to the new moon, yourself, and each other by visualizing what you are seeking. Feel into its arrival and joyously share the joys of it with yourself or the others in the group who are also helping to call it forth into the present.

On the second and third night of the new moon, whether you are working solo or in a group, everyone will be at their own locations for these final two nights of the new moon ritual. It is possible to gather on these nights if everyone can make it, and it feels aligned. If there is a group gathering on these two evenings, keep intensions clear and stay focused on the intentions of the sacred work.

On the second and third nights of the new moon, brew yourself and the new moon a cup of tea using your charged full moon water. Find a quiet place under the sky or near a window and light your black or purple candle. In your mind, experience the joy and fulfillment of your requests having manifested. Know that your candle is the new moon's direct path back to you.

Here is a chant you can use to further amplify your ritual on the second and third nights of the new moon:

Calling forth the things I (we) seek by candlelight.

I (we) share this tea under the new moon at night.

Receptive to clear answers, and thankful for clear sight.

Over the next thirteen days the moon will wax again, regaining its strength and size, representing the bounty she brings to you and your group.

In these next two weeks as the moon makes her way back to its abundant silvery orb in the sky, keep an open mind, remain curious and grateful, and pay attention to synchronicities and insights that may come through.

Know in your heart, the moon will bring you what you asked for. The physical manifestation of your desires might not look exactly like you thought they would, for they may arrive in unexpected shape, form, or opportunity. When these gifts arrive give thanks to the moon and give thanks to the harmony and power of a cup of tea.

Rejoice in the power of tea magic!

The Next Full Moon

In the days leading up to the full moon blooming, as she releases her gifts, be sure to contact the others in the group and share with them what has arrived.

If you are solo, make a note or write down what has opened for you in your life, what you have been guided to and what has been gifted to you. If you are working in a group, especially if it is the same group as your most recent moon rituals, come together on the next full moon. Dress for tea in the same fashion as you did for your prior full moon tea ritual, in colors of white, silver, cream, and light grey.

Prepare tea for yourself or the group with the water that was charged the previous full moon. Collectively remember what it is you wrote on the paper. Enjoy the magic of tea together, and honor and give thanks to the full moon.

Now, it is time to open the piece of paper that you had written your request on, during the previous full moon cycle. Lay the paper out in the moonlight. Review the contents and make note of what has arrived. Sing praises of gratitude to the blessings of the full moon. Hold gratitude in your heart, on your lips and in your mind. You can conclude this full-moon-to-new-moon-to-full-moon tea meditation by releasing the paper by burning it or by tearing it into tiny pieces and letting the wind carry it away.

A decision will need to be made to either continue this three-part moon ritual with yourself, the same group, or perhaps a new group. Whatever choice feels right for you, be sure to add new intentions on the full moon and prepare to collaborate with her in guiding them back to you on the forthcoming new moon.

As always, gratefully acknowledge the gifts when they arrive.

Next Steps with Moon Magic

With the moon cycles coming and going each month, this is a ritual that can be engaged in once a month, quarterly, or even yearly. Remember, though, this tea and moon magic ritual takes dedication. You must drink tea every night as the moon goes from full to dark and then back to full again. I also recommend establishing both short-term and long-term desires and goals to intersperse with the moon's cycles, and that both anchor and fuel your bigger desires.

While ancient in practice, moon magic was not always looked upon favorably. Thankfully, what was once considered punishable by death is now widely celebrated and openly practiced in most parts of the world. Weekend retreats, online courses, and entire books have been developed and written on the moon's cycles and how to interact with them.

Like most fundamental practices of Divine magic and that of tea witchery, while their popularity has grown in recent years, they are less of a trend, and more of a divinely timed resurgence of ancient practices that have been passed down for generations. These practices have been changed, added to, and built on for generations, and now, they are available to you.

Even if you have no one nearby you feel called to engage with an in-person group, these rituals can be done virtually via video conferencing. While video conferencing cannot replace the power of in-person gatherings, in today's world, it may be the best method for working with tea rituals and moon magic with groups.

Whether you are alone, connected with a group virtually, or engaging with others in person, tea rituals and moon magic go hand in heart as a potent combination for manifesting your dreams and desires.

Chapter 12

Zodiac Tea

Since the dawn of time, the cosmos has stirred the imaginations of billions of souls on Earth, as each new generation turns their gaze upward, seeking insight and longing for answers as to our place in the universe. What is it that we see when we look up but an incalculable cluster of twinkling stars and planetary bodies, each of them reflecting to us a map of the heavens? It is this celestial map, discovered in the placement and alignment of the stars and planets themselves, that reveals not just the inner workings of the universe, but also the inner workings of our own "innerverse."

The stars and our neighboring planets have not only been a powerful source of inspiration for every culture, but they have served as a guiding light for navigating daily life on Earth. Yes, people for centuries have looked up and made a wish upon a star, but even more than that, the stars and planets have served as infallible navigation on both sea and land, while signifying energetic shifts in the seasons, which have proven to be invaluable for agriculture.

I have been fascinated with astrology and astronomy ever since I can remember. Still, to this day, looking upward conjures a myriad of wonders, and stokes the fire of my imagination. Each time I stare into the worlds beyond our own, I am reminded of the famous nursery rhyme "Twinkle, twinkle little star, how I wonder what you are."

For me, the foundational state necessary for unlocking the mysteries of the universe and understanding what the stars and planets are communicating is to approach them with child-like curiosity and wonder. Thankfully, we are not alone in approaching them in this way, for we have centuries of cultures and brilliant individuals who took their curiosity and wonder, mixed in a blend of spiritual, intellectual, and scientific applications, and from this we have the multi-faceted disciplines of astronomy and astrology.

We also have the zodiac.

Understanding the Basics

You may be familiar with the zodiac and its corresponding energies and traits, particularly as it relates to your specific sign. If you are a professional psychic reader, or dabble in Divine magical practices, there is a good chance you are well versed in the zodiac. Wherever you may find yourself in your understanding of the zodiac, what I am sharing with you here will be helpful in your use of tea magic with the zodiac.

When it comes to understanding the stars and planets, there are two basic camps, one known as astronomy, and the other as astrology. Although both sides are looking at the same thing, their perspective and how they interpret what they see are quite different. This chapter is not designed to frame either perspective as more right or wrong to the other. Instead, you will be introduced to the correspondences between the twelve signs of the zodiac and the ideal teas to blend during those months. Understanding the basics makes it easier to work with tea and herbs on a planetary and astrological level.

We will start by looking at how the planets and stars, with their specific alignments during the zodiac, deliver a direct and distinct effect on the flora that grow on Earth. There are many ways to blend magical combinations of teas and botanicals. They all become much easier, fun, and more magically potent when you know how to sync your zodiac sign with the rhythm of flora, bringing their magical properties and spiritual and health benefits into your teacup.

Zodiac Flora

The stars, like the moon and sun, are always present, and always influencing our day-to-day lives. The planets in our solar system dance seamlessly among them, shining on and enchanting not only the skies above but those of us below the clouds as well.

Below the clouds include the flora.

In this case, I am speaking of the botanical flora that grows around the world, under the stars, absorbing all the sunlight, moonshine, celestial, and astronomical influences provided by the wonders of the cosmos and our atmosphere. When you sync your zodiac sign with the rhythm of flora you will find the most amazing, magical benefits, and allies in these plants and in your teacup.

There are many ways to blend magical combinations of teas and botanicals. Each botanical has a lore of its own, and each botanical has a planetary association with it. Once you understand them it is easy to blend teas with certain herbs and botanicals that are specifically aligned with your zodiac sign and astrological birth chart.

You can blend these botanicals to create a healing brew or potion for your health or for the health of others. You can also blend teas and herbs that align with a person's birthdate and zodiac sign to give a deeper tea leaf reading. The way you would do this is using herbs, teas, and botanicals that resonate specifically with that person, or a particular date in time such as a wedding anniversary, a past event, or a future event.

Tea, Herbs, and the Zodiac

In this section, you will find a brief description of the twelve zodiac signs, with their corresponding tea, planets, and herbs. We will start with Aries and conclude with Pisces.

Aries the Ram (March 21–April 19)

Aries is a fire sign ruled by the planet Mars. This cardinal fire sign is great at coming up with new ideas, a headfirst kind of person who rarely backs down from a challenge. Plants that grow in the time of Aries tend to have thorns or prickles. They can be fresh, spicy, or bitter in flavor. Aries rules the head, eyes, and face. Black tea is a strong and bold cup of tea for the Aries. It is straightforward and stands the test of time and integrity, just like the Ram. Adding a little ginseng or cayenne to this tea can give the Ram that extra bit of fiery follow-through that can help them bring their ideas to fruition. Herbs that correspond best in teas for Aries include nettles, cayenne, red clover, St. John's wort, marjoram, milk thistle, wormwood, sarsaparilla, tarragon, ginseng, rose, coriander, clove, and chamomile.

Taurus the Bull (April 20–May 20)

Taurus is an earth sign ruled by the planet Venus. Venus is the planet that represents desire, beauty, and luxury. They like to partake in fine foods and spirits. Those with Taurus as their sign are very practical, hardworking, patiently finish what they start, and revel in their success.

Plants that grow in the time of Taurus tend to be lush with beautiful flowers and foliage.

Taurus rules the throat and ears; therefore, the best plants for the Bull are often soothing to the throat or may calm the digestive system.

Rooibos herbal tea is flavorful and grounding for Taurus. This tea is associated with digestive wellness and high in antioxidants, which is perfect for keeping the Bull healthy. Adding a bit of lavender or anise to the rooibos will help those born under the Bull sign stay relaxed, easing the stubbornness that is sometimes associated with this sign.

Herbs that correspond best in teas for Taurus include licorice, fenugreek, slippery Elm, anise hyssop, lavender, dandelion, marshmallow, sage, feverfew, rooibos, thyme, angelica, and yarrow.

Gemini the Twins (May 21–June 20)

Ruled by the planet Mercury, Gemini is a mutable air sign. This allows them to maneuver into many places and adapt to new situations with relative ease. They can sometimes take on two personalities, one of the social butterfly, and the other as the creative, moody artist. This sometimes gives the illusion of them thinking they can be in two places at once, which can cause them to overbook and take on too many projects at once.

Plants that grow in the time of Gemini usually have finely divided stems and leaves, to represent the perceived two sides of them.

Being an air sign, they rule the lungs, shoulders, arms, and hands. Plants associated with Gemini help to strengthen the lungs and respiratory system or relax the nervous system.

Matcha green tea helps to bring focused balance to Geminis while keeping them alert and productive. This tea brings synergetic balance to the Twins. Using lemon balm in a brew for the Gemini helps reduce negative moods and promotes calmness for those born under this sign.

Herbs that correspond best in teas for Gemini include mullein, hyssop, lemon balm, lobelia, vervain, woodbine, yarrow, meadowsweet, fennel, skullcap, lavender, licorice, valerian, ashwagandha, and matcha.

Cancer the Crab (June 21–July 22)

Cancer is a water sign and is ruled by the moon. Cancerians can be very emotional and highly intuitive. They are very protective of their feelings, have a mysterious air about them, and are fiercely loyal to loved ones and friends.

Plants and vegetation that grow in the time of the Crab usually have soft, round, or moon-shaped leaves. They contain abundant moisture or are found near water. Oftentimes, they are white in color or have white or pale-yellow flowers.

Cancer rules the stomach, breasts, diaphragm, and liver, so plants that aid digestion or affect the subconscious are associated with the astrological sign of the Crab.

Jasmine green tea aligns with the Cancer sign. This tea brings harmony to emotional states and aligns the intuition of those born under this sign with their communication. Because of this, jasmine tea soothes the Crab while it nurtures their intuition. Peppermint tea also helps to ease the nervous feeling in the stomach Cancers sometimes feel.

Herbs that correspond best in teas for Cancer include peppermint, spearmint, papaya leaf, agrimony, lemon balm, parsley, verbena, chickweed, jasmine, sage, blood root, and green tea.

Leo the Lion (July 23–Aug. 22)

Leo is a fire sign that is ruled by the brilliant illumination of the sun. Those born under the sign of Leo are comfortable leading, and thus, standing out in both the celestial kingdom and the proverbial jungles of Earth. They thrive in the spotlight and are usually bursting with energy, enthusiasm, and ambition. Leos rule the heart, the most vital organ, and the center of the body.

Plants and vegetation associated with the sign of Leo are generally large and gold or orange in color or have heart-shaped leaves. Plants that regulate blood pressure and have an uplifting effect on the spirit are most beneficial to Leo.

A relaxing cup of chamomile and catnip tea will help soothe and calm the restless kitty. Pu-erh tea and hibiscus flavors this tea, making this flower combination a perfect blend for the heart-centered wisdom of the Leo. The rich and decadent pu-erh tea, coupled with the vibrant red and tangy zing of the hibiscus flower, brings great joy to the king of the jungle, keeping them in good and stable moods.

Herbs that correspond best in teas for Leo include borage, sunflower petals, rosemary, calendula, fennel, chamomile, hibiscus, dandelion, eyebright, ginger, saffron, red rose, and catnip.

Virgo the Virgin (Aug. 23–Sept. 22)

Virgo is an earth sign ruled by the planet Mercury. Highly analytical, Virgos tend to choose reason over emotions. They are exceedingly kind, logical, and hardworking and pay close attention to details in how they work and in the way they live their day-to-day lives.

Virgo is associated with the fall. Plants and vegetation associated with the sign of Virgo, then, are plants harvested for sustenance throughout the winter to come. These include all grains of wheat, barley oats, and rye.

Virgo is a centered human being who rules the abdomen, digestive system, and spleen. The most beneficial plants for those born under the sign of Virgo are plants that help to calm the nerves and release anxious thoughts.

White tea and lemongrass are beneficial to Virgos. The subtle strength and purity of white tea with its refreshing, mentally uplifting qualities of lemongrass, brings harmony and comfortable peace for Virgos.

Herbs that correspond best in teas for Virgo include fennel, blackberry leaves, chamomile, parsley, valerian, lavender, marjoram, licorice root, lemongrass, cannabis indica, catnip, and white tea.

Libra the Scales (Sept. 23–Oct. 22)

Libra is an air sign ruled by the planet Venus, the planet of beauty and love. Those born under this sign enjoy balance in all forms. Libras are the peacekeepers of the family. They are also sensual and highly romantic.

Plants associated with the sign of Libra often have light, lovely flowers, with deep scents. Libra rules the skin, kidneys, and adrenals, so plants and vegetation under this sign helps to cleanse and bring balance to these areas of the body.

Oolong tea is the perfect tea for Libras. This is because, like the balance of their sign, oolong tea is a perfect balance of green and black tea. Adding sensual rose, jasmine, and orange to oolong tea blends beautifully to suit the romantic tastes of the Libra.

Herbs that correspond best in teas for Libra include bergamot, meadowsweet, cornflowers, red rose, rose hips, mint, thyme, clove, elderberry, catnip, jasmine, and sweet orange.

Scorpio the Scorpion (Oct. 23–Nov. 21)

Scorpio is a water sign ruled by both Mars and Pluto. Scorpios are strong-willed, charming, magnetic, and emotional people. They are very resourceful and passionate.

Plants associated with Scorpio often grow under adversity. Nothing seems to keep them from growing and surviving, even the threat of looming winter.

The reproductive organs are ruled by Scorpio, so plants that balance the hormones, regulate the menstrual cycle, or help with childbirth and pregnancy are beneficial to Scorpio women. For men born under the sign of Scorpio, plants associated with prostate health and well-being are beneficial.

Although it is not necessarily a tea, yerba maté is an intense plant that delivers a healthy zing of caffeine for the Scorpion. This plant packs a powerful bitter, sometimes sour-sweet flavor. Since Scorpios like to stand out, yerba maté, when blended with ginger or stevia leaf, is an all-around winner for these individuals.

Herbs that correspond best in teas for Scorpio include ginseng, pennyroyal, raspberry leaf, saw palmetto, red clover, basil, wormwood, ginger, coriander, nettle, yerba maté, and stevia leaf.

Sagittarius the Archer (Nov. 22–Dec. 21)

Sagittarius is a fire sign ruled by the large and optimistic planet Jupiter. Lovers of the new and interesting make Sagittarians knowledge seekers who love to travel. They are born dreamers with an appetite for excitement.

Plants and vegetation associated with the celestial Archer tend to be large and leafy. The best plants for Sagittarius will support the eyesight, strengthen the sciatica and hips, and will promote a positive frame of mind.

Chai tea is ideally suited for those born under the sign of Sagittarius. It is a warm spicy black tea that lends cheer to the spirit, and warmth to a smile. Chai is a beloved worldly tea, and like the Sagittarius, it holds layers of flavor and texture.

Herbs that correspond best in teas for Sagittarius include passionflower, cinnamon, feverfew, sage, anise, nutmeg, lemon balm, calendula, ginger, black pepper, cannabis sativa, and black tea.

Capricorn the Climbing Goat (Dec. 22–Jan. 19)

Capricorns are an earth sign ruled by the planet Saturn. Capricorns are well grounded and viewed as responsible and loving people. They tend to be motivated and ambitious, though they also seek quiet space to hear themselves think.

Plants associated with Capricorn usually have few flowers and are woody, tough plants with long, slow growth that seem to somehow make it through the winter.

Capricorn rules the knees, joints, bones, and teeth, so as a result, plants that are high in calcium can be greatly beneficial for the Climbing Goat.

Earl Grey tea is perfect for the Capricorn. It is classic, not too fussy, easy to access, and holds the power of wellness and sophistication. Sarsaparilla and cardamon help to warm up the Capricorn to keep them friendly and upbeat.

Herbs that correspond best in teas for Capricorn include comfrey, sarsaparilla, kava kava, thyme, tormentil, bergamot, cardamom, vanilla, rosemary, cannabis indica, chamomile, lemon, and ginger.

Aquarius the Water Bearer (Jan. 20–Feb. 18)

Aquarius is an air sign ruled by the planet Uranus. Aquarians are deep thinkers and are known to be highly intellectual beings. They thrive in social situations and adore the ones they love and are close to, lavishing them with attention and gifts.

Plants associated with the Water Bearer seem to live on air, often thriving in the desert. The most healing and beneficial plants for those born under the sign of Aquarius are ones that help circulation, relax the nervous system, or promote inspiration.

Green tea makes an excellent cup of tea for the Aquarius. This tea promotes focus and inner peace, allowing the Aquarian to harmonize their analytical thoughts with their meditative moments.

Herbs that correspond best in teas for Aquarius include chamomile, catnip, skullcap, rosemary, valerian, gingko biloba, kava kava, cinnamon, and fennel.

Pisces the Fishes (Feb. 19–March 20)

Pisces is a water sign ruled by both Jupiter and Neptune. Pisces seem to alternate between reality and the dream world, and due to this, they are known for having highly attuned intuition. They make the greatest friends and are sensitive to their own feelings as well as to the feelings of others around them. Those born under the sign of Pisces tend to be more appreciative of life's lessons than most.

Plants and vegetation associated with Pisces often grow near the ocean. These types of plants, which can survive stormy climates, are ideal for the Fishes.

The most healing plants for them are those that strengthen the immune and nervous system or have an antibacterial and antiviral effect. Pisces plants may also catalyze and expand higher states of awareness and consciousness, which can be helpful in dream work.

Yellow tea is perfectly aligned for Pisces. Smooth and precise, this tea lends joy and creativity to its drinkers. This allows the Pisces to communicate on a complex and sophisticated level, bringing deep and meaningful conversation when talking to friends and family.

Herbs that correspond best in teas for Pisces include golden seal, echinacea, eyebright, mugwort, kava kava, yarrow, skullcap, oat straw, nutmeg, anise, five finger grass, and psilocybin mushrooms.

Next Steps with Your Tea Journey

By this point in your journey with tea witchery, it goes without saying that regardless of your astrological sign, tea magic is a year-round endeavor, and you can drink any tea or potion your heart desires at any time. That said, if you are looking at working with the zodiac, either for your own personal journeys or if it is part of your professional practice for doing readings for others, having a basic understanding of teas, tisanes, and herbal potions makes it much simpler to incorporate the astrological charts.

So, where do you go from here? Unless you are a well-seasoned Kitchen Witch, I would recommend your next steps with the zodiac begin with the basics.

An ideal place to start is to get to know more about the nuances and energy patterns of the four seasons: spring, summer, fall, and winter. These times of year greatly affect all vegetation and determine their growth cycle. For instance, when you think of spring, you think of new beginnings and fresh growth. This can be related to people born in the spring, with the sign of Aries, who are invigorated by new ideas, and function at their best when beginning new things. Winter people such as Capricorns tend to be filled with a strong sense of family, and are more drawn to comfort, practicality, and stability to weather storms.

One enjoyable act of preparation for weaving together your tea magic with the zodiac is to spend a year collecting herbs and tea each month for each sign. Store them in an airtight container and keep your teas and herbs out of the sunlight. In one year, you will have an apothecary of twelve tea blends to share with your friends and family. You can use them for wellness, and you can use them to give deeper insight to teacup scrying, tea leaf reading, and conjuring spells in your teacup cauldron.

The plants and vegetation that grow directly in the month of the astrological sign serve as ideal ingredients for your tea when working with the zodiac. While certain teas and herbs I have associated with the star signs are greatly beneficial to health, wellness, and magic for that sign, they also can bring the same or similar results for the other zodiac signs. Keeping this in mind, I encourage you to blend your own brews, be creative and resourceful, and do your homework, but most of all trust your intuition when working with the plants and the celestial realm.

Chapter 13

Understanding Cannabis Tea

The cannabis plant is as diverse as it is controversial. The culturally rich history of cannabis has been dated as far back as 12,000 years in what is now Mongolia and southern Siberia, although other researchers place its initial discovery in Asia round 300 BC.[27] Regardless of its date of origins, two things all researchers agree on with cannabis is that it has gone by many different names and remains one of the most versatile plants and crops in human history.

The cannabis planet can grow and flourish in nearly every possible climate. For most of its history, cannabis has been cultivated and used for the unparalleled strength and versatility of its fibers. From its use in building materials, including rope, fishnets, and clothing, to oils and fuel, there are few plants known to have benefited humanity as cannabis has.

There has also been much evidence discovered throughout history revealing cannabis was widely used medicinally, to ease pain and stomach aches, reduce nausea, and induce sleep. While studying in India in the 1830s, an Irish doctor by the name of Sir William Brook O'Shaughnessy discovered that cannabis tinctures

---

27. Blaszcka, "How One Plant Spread through the World."

and infusions had been previously used for many years throughout India and Asia to treat many of the aforementioned ailments.[28]

It is understood that this same doctor also brought this helpful information about cannabis to the Western countries of Europe and to the Americas. During this time cannabis found its place in the gardens of kitchen witches and healers, where it was brewed into folk remedies, ranging from poultices to tea.[29]

By the end of the eighteenth century, physicians and pharmacists were prescribing cannabis infusions, tinctures, and extracts throughout Europe and the United States to cure and help alleviate painful symptoms from a host of illnesses and physical atrocities. In fact, the more controversial reputation cannabis has garnered is a new, modern creation that has little in common with how most of the world viewed and used this remarkable plant throughout history.[30]

It was not until the Prohibition era of the 1920s and 1930s that cannabis was lumped in with alcohol as being illegal in the United States. From that point, until recently, cannabis could no longer be prescribed medicinally, and was considered addictive and led to uncontrollable behavior.

Today, we find ourselves amid a cannabis revolution. People are starting to realize and accept the vast array of medicinal benefits of cannabis that are far more helpful than harmful. Cannabis is being re-evaluated and prescribed more frequently and openly as a complementary medicinal component in pain management.

Three Major Strains and How They Work

Indica, sativa, and hemp are the three major strains of the cannabis plant. There are two main medicinal compounds in these cannabis plants: CBD and THC. Through modern technology, we have discovered how the strains of this plant, along with a myriad of its health and medicinal benefits, can be broken down, analyzed, and prescribed for each of their unique benefits.

28. "Marijuana." History.com.

29. Ibid.

30. "History of Marijuana as Medicine: 2900 BC to Present." BrittanicaProCon.org.

• *CBD (Cannabidiol):* The CBD compound has been shown to relieve inflammation, anxiety, and restlessness, along with helping ease pain.

• *THC (Tetrahydrocannabinol):* THC compound produces the psycho-active substance which leaves the mind feeling sleepy, woozy, cloudy, and relaxed.

With modern advancements, the cannabis plants can be specifically grown for these two compounds. CBD and THC can be separated and used separately to aid in health and healing. This takes us back to the current revolution of the cannabis plant as CBD has taken the alternative medicine world by storm, making it a much sought-after complement to other medical regimes.

There are three primary strains of cannabis that are used medicinally and in industry. These strains are where the THC and CBD are extracted from. The strains carry both THC and CBD, although the levels vary from plant to plant and can be higher in one compound and lower in the other, thus producing different effects.

Cannabis Sativa

The use of this flower, extract, or tincture tends to give a boost of energy and facilitates clear focus. It also helps reduce inflammation, ease pain, and uplift anxiety.

Cannabis Indica

Using this strain of flower, extract, or tincture is excellent for inducing sleep and increasing appetite. It also aids in easing pain, soothing muscle spasms, and relaxing tension.

Cannabis Hemp

This strain has the lowest amount of THC. CBD compound can be derived from hemp. Hemp has mostly been used in the industrial sect to manufacture fiber.

If the cannabis plant grows THC and CBD at the same time, in the same plant, that should be respected and used as Mother Nature intended it. These two compounds are most effective when used together, especially in your tea.

Tea with Cannabis

It would be wonderful if all you must do to brew your tea with cannabis is to place the cannabis in hot water and BINGO you have relaxing tea! It is, however, a little trickier than that. Cannabis in plain hot or boiling water has little to no medicinal effect at all.

To properly activate the THC and CBD in the cannabis, you must decarboxylate it first. I know this sounds all big and scientific, but it is not as hard as it may seem. There are a couple ways to do it. I am going to share with you the most simple and direct way to do it for tea. I would venture to say that it is the first and oldest way of activation. So, let us trust our ancestors and brew it up their way. In the process, I will explain how decarboxylation works, and how to do it all while making tea.

Pick the type of cannabis strain you want to use and grind it down or break it up into smaller pieces. You may want to research and add the extra benefits of other herbs such as peppermint, lavender, and cinnamon. The herbs you choose can add benefits to your tea; it will enhance its medicinal benefits, and it will elevate the flavor of the tea.

THC, CBD, Strains, and How They Work

Deep Relaxation Cannabis Tea

This recipe yields four cups or one pot of tea. Here is what you'll need:

4 cups of water

½ cup of whole milk. If you are dairy free you can use 2 tablespoons of coconut oil. (Milk should be room temperature or warmed before adding to brew.)

¼ cup of all-natural honey (*Optional*)

1 tablespoon spearmint

1 tablespoon catnip

1 teaspoon chamomile

½ teaspoon lavender

　■　2 grams of finely shredded cannabis

　■　1 (3 x 5) drawstring muslin bag

Place all dry ingredients into a large brewing bag, so there is room for the water to flow through the bag and the herbs have room to expand, releasing all their goodness into your brew.

You can get reusable 3x5 or larger drawstring muslin bags at most health food stores, and online.

Bring four cups of water to a vigorous boil. Place the bag in the boiling water and allow to boil for three minutes. This is an important part of decarboxylation that gets the trichomes, the crystals from the leaves of the plant, and activates the THC and CBD. Do not over boil as it should be three to four minutes only. Then reduce heat to low.

Now that the trichomes have been removed and are invisibly floating around in your tea water, they need something to adhere to; particularly, they need a fat of some sort. When you reduce the heat to low, add ½ cup of whole milk or real milk cream, such as half and half, to the teapot and let it simmer for fifteen minutes before serving.

The fat from the milk allows the trichomes to be carried into your bloodstream and then releases the beneficial compounds of THC and CBD into your system, easing you into that relaxed state of pain-free wellness that cannabis is famous for.

Using high heat and a fat soluble, such as milk or butter, is the most common way to release and activate the THC and CBD. Coconut oil works and so does olive oil; they are just not as fatty as good old-fashioned whole milk. If you add too much oil your tea becomes oily and less appetizing.

Using honey instead of a fat or oil when making tea also has been shown to activate the THC and CBD by adhering to it and then carrying it to your blood stream. This method can cause the tea to be overly sweet and may not be as strong as milk fat.

Drinking medicinal cannabis tea is a much healthier alternative than smoking cannabis because you are not breathing in all the carcinogens in the plant matter and exposing your lungs to harsh heat and smoke.

One very important thing you should know about ingesting cannabis is that it takes a little longer to reach your system. If your stomach is full of food, it may take even longer to work its way through the digestive tract and into your bloodstream. So be prepared to relax and allow it to take its course. It could take up to two hours or longer to start feeling the effects. After drinking this tea, you should not drive or operate machinery.

Cannabis Chai Tea

Cannabis chai tea is a beautiful warm and relaxing way to experience the pain-reliving benefits of cannabis in tea form. Since chai is traditionally a milk-based tea, it might be something more familiar and palatable to try when first introducing cannabis to your tea.

This recipe also gives you the added pick-me-up benefits of caffeine that help to balance out the mellow woozy feeling of the THC in the cannabis. Yields six cups of tea or one large pot. Here is what you will need:

5 cups water

2 cups whole milk (or 2 cups of whole chocolate milk)

¼ cup of honey

¼ cup black tea

3 grams finely ground cannabis

2 tablespoons vanilla extract

1 tablespoon powdered cinnamon

2 teaspoons ground black pepper

1 teaspoon powdered cardamom

1 teaspoon powdered clove

1 teaspoon ground ginger

1 (4 x 6) drawstring muslin bag

Bring five cups of water, honey, and vanilla extract to a rapid boil. Place all dry ingredients into muslin bag. Cinch closed and tie in a bow.

Place bag into boiling honey water for three to five minutes, allowing the water to vigorously boil with that bag in the pot. Reduce heat to low and add the milk. Let simmer for another fifteen minutes before serving.

If you are using whole cinnamon sticks, cloves, and cardamom pods, you will need to use triple the amount and allow it to simmer and steep an additional ten to fifteen minutes longer in the water, honey, milk, and vanilla brew. If using fresh ginger, keep in mind it may get hotter and spicier if you use too much.

Enjoy one to two cups slowly to see how this will affect you. Also, remember not to drive or operate heavy machinery when under the influence of cannabis tea.

Next Steps with Cannabis Tea

Modern opinions are rapidly changing about the cannabis plant. Many have realized that the medicinal values of this plant are much safer to use than some pharmaceuticals, not to mention it is also quite a bit less expensive. To get your hands on the flowers to make cannabis tea, if you live in a cannabis friendly state, you can ask your local dispensary for advice on what strains of flowers to use. You might want to pick a cannabis flower that is fruity such as a strain called Cherry Pie, Grape Ape, or Sour Diesel. Use your own nose to decide what you like.

You can also ask your bud tender if the flower is low or high in CBD and THC. Spend some time talking about what you are trying to accomplish with this cup of tea.

Drinking cannabis tea will show up as a positive on any drug test. Please be sure to check your state or country guidelines, as well as your employer's guidelines, to see if this type of tea drinking is right for you and your lifestyle.

Chapter 14

What to Do with Tea Beyond Drinking It

If you have a passion for tea and herbs, it is not uncommon to find yourself in a situation of overabundance. At some point in time, we have all bought a tea or two that was not our favorite, but we cannot bring ourselves to throw them away. Another common situation is you have stockpiled teas over the years, only to realize some have gone way beyond their expiration date.

If you can relate and have wondered what to do with all those excess teas you will not drink, this final chapter is for you!

Bathing with Tea

In this section, I am going to share with you four teas that can produce amazing results for your mind, body, and spirit when applied to bathing.

Black Tea

Black tea reduces foot and palm sweats. This old-school remedy involves soaking the feet or hands in a basin of warm water with two black tea bags. The tannins in the tea close the pores in the skin, reducing sweating.

Brew the tea bags in hot water first, allowing the essence to seep into the water. Let the water to cool down or dilute to a comfortable temperature for soaking your feet. Allow sweaty feet to soak for twenty minutes at a time.

Cooling Mint

Soaking the feet in a mixture of peppermint tea and lemon improves blood circulation, which both soothes and boosts the nervous system.

At night, when you soak your feet in this mixture, you benefit from the changes occurring in your body, and you feel more energetic in the morning.

You may also use spearmint, winter mint, and citrus peels.

Chamomile Bath

A cool bath with chamomile tea is wonderful if you have sensitive skin, and you are experiencing rash or bug bites. Chamomile will calm skin irritations such as redness and itchiness. Chamomile will also leave your skin feeling smooth and refreshed.

Green Tea

Green tea is a popular choice for a bath soak, as it can help reduce muscle pain. Green tea is also soothing and softening for the skin, helping to relieve redness. Green tea is loaded with antioxidants, making a green tea soak a wonderful way for you to benefit from anti-aging effects. Green tea also helps your skin to recover from environmental irritants and can pull excess toxins from your skin and pores.

Alternative Uses of Teas

In this section, I am going to share with you a variety of healthy and rejuvenating alternative uses of tea.

Exfoliant

Grind up or finely cut loose-leaf tea. Add to a mild body wash to create an energizing and exfoliating effect for the skin and body. You can also create your own scrub by adding finely cut or ground tea to a sugar or salt scrub.

Make Potpourri

Place scented tea leaves and dried flowers in small containers or dishes to add fragrance and decoration to a room. Place these dishes by a bed, in an office, waiting rooms, or in the bathroom. Combining tea leaves and dried flowers is easy and works like a charm.

Invigorating Body Oil

Start by placing about a half cup of desired tea and herbs into a quart jar. Fill jar with one cup extra virgin olive oil, one cup grapeseed oil, and one cup avocado seed oil.

Place the jar in the dark for fifteen days. Shake vigorously for ten to fifteen seconds every three days. This will allow the herbs and tea to infuse into the oils. Strain out plant matter and put a lid on it. Keep it stored out of sunlight.

This tea and body oil recipe is helps relieve dry skin and itchy, dull skin. It can do wonders when added to a warm bath or applied after the shower. Be creative and experiment by adding different drops of essential oils, tea, and herbs.

Uplifting Body Spray

Brew up some mint-based or floral tea such as peppermint, spearmint, jasmine, or rose. Allow this tea to go to room temperature, then pour into a spray bottle and place it in the refrigerator for at least three hours. Using tea as a room spray with added magical intent, such as the right corresponding water and herbs, can clear energy and add an element of magical power to the room. This blend also works perfectly as a cooling body mist when you step out of the shower. It is also a nice hair mist that adds a fragrant cooldown when you are feeling overheated.

Floor and Furniture Refresher

Use a dark tea and be sure to steep it for hours. Use green tea for lighter woods such as bamboo, pine, and wicker. Dip a rag in and rub the dark tea on your hardwood floors or furniture to draw out color. This method and use of dark tea will help even the color and give a natural shine to the wood. Whether you choose to use a dark tea or green tea, both are excellent for maintaining an earth-friendly hardwood floor and furniture.

Tea Staining

To make natural fabrics and paper appear to have an antique feel, brew up an extraordinarily strong pan of tea. Place garment into pot and let sit for up to twenty minutes, depending on how dark you would like the staining or antiquing to be. Allow garment to air dry before washing it to set the stain. To set the stain even deeper, after the garment is dry, place it in a white vinegar bath for ten minutes before washing.

Deodorizer

Tea as a deodorizer has many uses. You can put dry unused tea bags in your fridge to soak up rotten smells. This also works in closets, lockers, and cars. Try using Earl Grey, jasmine, mint, or other scented teas to add an uplifting essence and welcoming scent in your home, office, waiting areas, bathrooms, gyms, and garages.

Treat Dark Eye Circles

After you have enjoyed your tea, reuse the damp tea bags that have excess tea squeezed out of them. Place the tea bags in the refrigerator for up to an hour or longer. After that, use the cold tea bags for treating dark circles under your eyes by applying them over your eyelids for fifteen to twenty minutes.

Compost and Garden Tea

To promote healthy plants, you can use discarded tea leaves in your compost and garden. Do not discard non-biodegradable tea bags with string and stapled paper into your compost.

Conclusion

Next Steps with Tea Magic

Now that you have completed the chapters of *Tea Magic*, what is next?

For starters, I encourage you to visit the Directory of Correspondences, which follows this chapter. What was originally going to be a chapter for this book turned into an extensive directory of tea and herbal correspondences that will be beneficial to all your tea witchery endeavors for years to come. Along with guidance on brewing your own potions, the directory offers up basic teas and their correspondences for you to explore in your unfolding journey with tea magic and kitchen witchery.

If you find yourself wanting to revisit certain chapters, I invite you to take notes in a tea witchery journal if you did not take notes the first time around. You may also be excited to get to the next level of tea witchery. But after completing the book, and with so many options at your disposal for engaging in tea magic, it is natural to feel a little overwhelmed with where to begin. So, let us revisit some of the basics.

Most of what you need to create tea magic and perform kitchen witchery are already in your own kitchen. As you learned earlier in the book, there are three important ingredients for creating magic through tea witchery, no matter what practice you are called to engage in:

1. First and foremost, is embodying the abundance of happiness.

2. Approaching life with an open mind and curiosity.

3. Trust the infallible guidance of your inner voice.

I believe having an abundance of happiness is the foundation to all things magical. When you embody happiness, things begin to grow, successes flourish, and the ideal people and opportunities are magnetized to you. You are attracting abundance and joy to you because you feel good to be around. This aids in attracting the things you desire in life. Happiness can move mountains, grow a business, a family, and friendships, and it can fill your life with magic and amazement.

I also invite you to embark on an open-minded journey to do further research on tea and the magical topics and practices you learned about within these pages. Start with what you have a deep curiosity and interest in. Remember, curiosity is one of the main ingredients to unlocking the magical properties and healing power of tea magic and kitchen witchery, both of which are inseparable.

In the case of kitchen witchery, or as some refer to it kitchen magic, this is a kind of magic that does not require fancy and rare herbs or tea supplies from far-off and exotic countries. So, there will always be opportunities for you to engage in and further explore the distinct characteristics, rituals, recipes, healing benefits, and history of all things tea witchery.

Most importantly, whether you are interacting with the living or dead through tea magic, always come from a place of love, respect, child-like curiosity, appreciation, and an abundance of happiness. For when you embody these high-vibrational qualities you will attract the energies of people, spirits, opportunities, and experiences that beautifully reflect your own well-intentioned desires to work with the physical and spirit world. As above, so below.

Appendix A

Directory of Correspondences

One of the easiest and most enjoyable ways to take charge of your health is to create your own tea blends. Whether you are a seasoned herbalist, a tea expert, a Kitchen Witch, or you are just starting out, the first step in learning is doing and trying your own healing and healthy tea potions.

In this Directory of Correspondences, you will receive a review on several correspondences with tea and herbs we covered in the book, along with many others.

It is safe to blend both tea and herbs together to create your desired effect or flavor. However, if you are taking medication prescribed by a doctor you should not replace that medication with an herbal or tea remedy. I also recommend that you check with a doctor or licensed pharmacist to see if any herbs or teas may have an adverse effect on the medication you are already taking. Herbal and tea therapy should be complementary medicine, not a substitution for medicine.

Blend Your Own Potions

Tisanes

Tisanes, often referred to as "herbal tea," are brewed herbs and flowers that are steeped in hot water to allow the transfer of their essences to infuse into the water or liquid. There is no actual tea in a tisane; therefore, they usually do not contain caffeine.

Decoctions

Decoctions are brews of hardier plant matter such as roots, barks, seeds, and stems that may require a lower brewing temperature and a longer steeping time. Chai often falls in this category due to the contents of cinnamon, ginger, and black pepper. These ingredients usually need a longer steep time not only to release flavor but to slowly break down into the water, giving a thicker texture to your brew.

Cold Infusion

Cold infusion is when you do not heat the liquid but allow the plant matter to sit in the liquid for several hours, days, or even weeks. It should be in a dark, cool place to allow the matter to slowly infuse and release its essences.

Tinctures

Tinctures are made by following the steps for cold infusion. Tincture is a concentrated infusion of the teas and medicinal plants that have been infused for long periods of time in a high alcohol base such as a premium vodka or an organic food-grade alcohol.

Tinctures are often stored for later use as they have a much longer shelf life being they have been infused into alcohol. When you have reached the desired strength strain out all the plant matter and store in a cool place out of the light. The tincture is then added to other teas or drinks for its medicinal benefits. If you can stand the flavor, you can drop it directly under your tongue for quick absorption of its benefits.

Perfumed

Perfumed means that the tea has been flavored by adding flower petals, fruits, spices, and/or natural and artificial concentrated oils and flavorings directly to the blend and stored in an airtight container which is opened and tossed about every few days to allow for proper mixing and saturation. The best perfumed teas take up to two to three weeks to cure and fully permeate the blend.

Teas, Herbs, and
Botanical Correspondences

Connecting with the basic teas and their correspondence at various points of your tea journey and exploration of tea magic is a good exercise for your taste pallet as well as a reminder of your how important it is to get to know tea as part of your magical endeavors.

Tea not only originated in China, but in 2020 China was still the largest producer and exporter of tea.[31] There are hundreds of tea-producing regions around the world including India, Sri Lanka, Kenya, Indonesia, and Argentina, to name a few.

Each region produces and processes its signature style, creating from exceedingly small to very distinguishable differences in tea flavor, color, and texture. I invite you to experience as many as possible to understand what flavor profile works best for your pallet, mood, healing, and magic.

Botanical and healing herbs can be sourced from regions around the world too. It is up to you to pick the best herbal and botanical matches for your specific purposes. For example, the lavender fields of France are said to produce the finest lavender, Bulgaria the best roses, and California the best cannabis.

Whether you are brewing a tisane, a tea, or a magical blend of your own, you must research, procure, or grow your own herbs to brew your potions and tea with, this will ensure that you have the best quality plant material to add to your teacup cauldron.

Herbs, flowers, roots, teas, and barks are perfect for incorporating aromatherapy and herbal therapy into your teacup meditation, healing possibilities, and ingestible potion work.

Here is a compilation of teas, botanicals, herbs, and flora that can be helpful when you are researching a healing or magical brew, potion, or cup of tea.

---

31. Ridder, "Leading Tea Exporters Worldwide 2021."

Correspondences

Allspice

Allspice has carminative properties which means it can relieve gas, bloating, and tummy aches. It may ease diarrhea, nausea, vomiting, bloating, and even constipation.

Correspondences for Allspice

Determination, harmony, energy, and fertility. Allspice also brings comfort to those in distress.

Angelica

Angelica can be used to ease heartburn and acid reflux. This botanical can aid in the slowing of dementia, calm anxiety, lessen nervousness, and help you sleep.

Correspondences for Angelica

Angelica is a guardian of creativity and attracts positive energy. This botanical can be used for protection against negativity and works well as a hex or jinx breaker.

Anise

Anise is an antibacterial that has anti-inflammatory properties and may fight stomach ulcers, keep blood sugar levels in order, and reduce symptoms of depression and menopause.

Correspondences for Anise

Love, protection, psychic abilities, purification, libido enhancer, and an ally in new moon work. This spice is said to ease nightmares and enhance protection when lucid dreaming is occurring.

Ashwagandha

Ashwagandha is a mood stabilizer and can ease stress and anxiety. This herb can stabilize blood sugar and ease sugar cravings. It can also help boost your immune system, aiding you to feel happy and rejuvenated.

Correspondences for Ashwagandha

Can strengthen spiritual well-being and bring balanced thinking. This is a powerful Ayurveda herb that can feed and nourish the body from the inside out, creating healthy muscles and skin.

Assam Black Tea

Assam black tea is the pride and joy of India. This is a rich, hardy black tea and makes for an excellent iced tea. Its health benefits include prolonged stamina and clear focus, and can lower blood pressure and increase blood flow to vital organs such as the heart, liver, and lungs. This tea is also well known for boosting energy and stamina, while also aiding in lowering blood pressure and promoting bone density and dental health.

Correspondences for Assam Black Tea

Productivity, protection, divination, spirit work, banishing, stability, power, and prosperity.

Basil

Basil eases headaches, earaches, and indigestion, and is an excellent source of vitamin K, manganese, iron, vitamin A, and vitamin C, calcium, and magnesium. With its delightful flavor, this herb is a beautiful accent in tea blends.

Correspondences for Basil

Love, peace, understanding, confidence, courage, and creativity. This herb can also soothe tempers and bring about peace.

Bay Leaves

Like basil, bay leaves contain high amounts of vitamins and minerals. Bay has a soothing and medicinal flavor when added to tea that can aid in digestion after meals and bring relaxation and calmness.

Correspondences for Bay Leaves

Healing, protection, psychic ability facilitator, repels negativity, protects, and wards off the evil eye and unwanted attention.

Black Pepper

Black pepper warms your body internally and prepares your body to take in and process other herbs and teas. Using black pepper in tea can help with coughs and sore throats according to Ayurveda medicine practices. Black pepper is one of the warming and spicy ingredients in a true Masala Chai tea.

Correspondences for Black Pepper

Banishing and clearing obstacles, protection of property, purification, adds spice and excitement to stale patterns and relationships.

Black Tea

The most common tea found in the US and British markets. This is the tea and flavor we think of when we think of Lipton tea. Black tea is produced in several countries around the world and is most often a blend of more than one tea from different regions.

Black tea contains more caffeine than its sister teas, such as green tea and white tea, while it contains a lower number of beneficial antioxidants. It will boost energy and stamina, aids in lowering blood pressure, helps promote bone density and dental health. Black tea is a full-bodied tea in terms of flavor with a rich and earthy taste. Malty, smoky, spiced, caramel, and floral notes can be detected in many black teas.

Correspondences for Black Tea

This is the same as it is for Assam black tea—Productivity, protection, divination, spirit work, banishing, stability, power, and prosperity.

Cacao

Cacao is rich in antioxidants and serves as a mood enhancer and mild stimulant. Cacao also gives you a guilt-free and calorie-free chocolaty pick-me-up.

Correspondences for Cacao

Cacao is used in love spells and sex magic. It is used to boost euphoria and is an excellent offering to a feminine deity.

Calendula Petals (Marigold)

Calendula petals promote wound and skin healing, and can cool down hot flashes and bring down fevers. It is an anti-inflammatory and can also bring down swelling and rashes in the skin. This flower aids in revitalizing skin and beauty.

Correspondences for Calendula Petals

Brings beauty and attracts lovers. This golden flower petal is often used when seeking prosperity and successes.

Cannabis

Cannabis acts as a sedative and a mood enhancer. This controversial but diverse plant has been known to increase appetite and lift depression. Cannabis is widely known to be a pain reliever and an anti-spasmatic which is helpful when dealing with deep-tissue injuries and pain.

Correspondences for Cannabis

Cannabis is used to facilitate deep trance like states when meditating and scrying. This plant can bring laughter and sexual arousal.

Caraway Seeds

Caraway seed tea is used to help alleviate digestive problems including heartburn, bloating, gas, loss of appetite, and mild spasms of the stomach and intestines.

Correspondences for Caraway Seeds

Caraway seeds are used in teas of protection and safekeeping. Aids in secret keeping, trust, and mental protection. These seeds are said to ensure safe travels.

Cardamom

Cardamom helps to flush out toxins and is a metabolism booter helping to aid in weight loss. Improves blood circulation and has anti-inflammatory compounds that can ease pain in muscles,and joints.

Correspondences for Cardamom

Increases strength of unions, love, friendships, and business partners. Cardamom aids in overall wellness, helps to keep harmony and peace, and can soothe broken hearts.

Catnip/Catmint

This herb can help ease restlessness, and reduce anxiety and nervousness. Catnip makes humans lazy and cats crazy. This is an excellent sleep inducer and mind relaxer.

Correspondences for Catnip

Catnip brings speediness to meditations and spell work. Catmint is often used in dream work such as lucid dreams and astral projection.

Cayenne Pepper / Chili Peppers

Cayenne pepper and chili peppers soothe coughs and colds, and acts as an expectorant to release phlegm from the lungs. Cayenne assists in alleviating nerve pain and arthritis.

Correspondences for Cayenne Pepper and Chili Peppers

Adds spice to relationships and power to sex magic. Chili peppers are often used to break hexes, curses, and to ward off the evil eye. Chili peppers release unwanted vibrations from your body and remove stuck and stagnant energy points in the body.

Chamomile

Chamomile is a mild sedative that can aid in the reduction of anxiety and stress. This herb makes an excellent tea before bed to calm the mind and relax the nervous system.

Correspondences for Chamomile

Chamomile helps to heighten focused energy and brings prosperous thoughts to your unconscious and conscious mind.

Chaste Tree Berries

Chaste tree berries have been used to treat menstrual cycle problems and pain, premenstrual syndrome, and menopause. Chaste tree berries may help stimulate progesterone. It is also known to help normalize estrogen and progesterone production, helping to soothe and ease pain and irritability associated with menstruation.

Correspondences for Chaste Tree Berries

Chaste tree berries are used for moon magic work and moon tea. They are also powerful for summoning goddesses and seeking their help in matters of fertility.

Chrysanthemum

Chrysanthemum is a cooling flower and is often drank in the summertime in China. This flower will help calm fatigue and combat respiratory illnesses.

Correspondences for Chrysanthemum

Often associated with the sun and used to represent fire, the chrysanthemum flower represents protection and should be planted around your home. Chrysanthemums are a natural flea and pest repellent when planted near your home. Crumble the dead flower heads around your doorways and windowsills.

Cinnamon Bark

Cinnamon bark is filled with powerful antioxidants and promotes many health benefits. It is an anti-inflammatory that can reduce pain and swelling in your muscles and deep tissues. This is also used for easing the pain of menstrual cramps and releases swelling. This bark can help to control your blood sugars by easing cravings for sweets that can help lead to weight loss.

Correspondences for Cinnamon Bark

Cinnamon bark raises your vibration to a higher state of consciousness and enhances psychic ability. It is often used to summons deities when applied as an incense or anointing oil. This bark brings money, success, and spiritual awakening. Cinnamon bark is also used to heighten sex magic, lust, and passion.

Citrus Peel

Citrus peel is high in vitamin C and helps the body to absorb nutrients. Citrus helps to uplift your mood and brings about happiness, which as I have shared throughout the book, is essential to manifesting your desired results with tea witchery.

Correspondences for Citrus Peel

Working with citrus peel elicits joy, inspiration, and abundance. Citrus peel can also help you clear away uneasy thoughts and peacefully end unhealthy relationships.

Clove

Clove soothes sore throats and coughs, and is an anti-inflammatory. Cloves help to ease tooth pain and can be a natural numbing agent.

Correspondences for Clove

Cloves are warm, inviting, and useful in summoning calm and peaceful meetings with others. They are known to bring courage, protection, and riches to those who work with them. Clove can also stop someone from gossiping about you.

Coconut

Coconut is rejuvenating and helps the body to maintain hydration. It is high in magnesium and aids in teeth and bone health.

Correspondences for Coconut

Coconut is used for purification and protection of chastity. It brings beauty, confidence, and flexibility. Nuts in general are also used in fertility potions.

Cornflower

Cornflower helps to ease headaches and congestion. Cornflower also may contain antibiotic and antioxidant properties that can act as a preventative for warding off illnesses, such as the common cold.

Correspondences for Cornflower

Cornflower is used to heal the third eye and balance mental clarity and psychic visions. Cornflower is also useful in bringing peace to a work environment and the home.

Damiana

Damiana is an anti-depressant that has an uplifting and stimulating effect on the mind and body. Damiana is said to be an aphrodisiac, helping to bring sex drive back to both women and men.

Correspondences for Damiana

Damian is used for lust potions, and is applicable for love, sex, and passion magic work. Damiana also brings forth visions and lucid dreams.

Dandelions

Dandelions are detoxifying and cleansing to the body by aiding in digestion and helping to relieve constipation.

Correspondences for Dandelions

Dandelions are useful for divination, as well aswish and spirit calling. When the dandelion root is roasted and brewed into tea this is said to bring psychic visions and answers. This tea sat by your bed side, while you sleep, will bring answers from loved ones who have crossed over.

Darjeeling Tea

Darjeeling is produced in India and is in a class of its own. There are many layers to this fine and delicate tea. Processing this tea yields white tea, green tea, and black tea. Darjeeling teas are known as the "Champagne of Teas" and are revered for their flavor, vibrancy, and superiority. There are many layers to this delicate tea, with Darjeeling tea having been established as a very fine supreme tea with crisp citrus notes and a floral finish.

Correspondences for Darjeeling Tea

Health and vitality and are powerful aids when meditating on prosperity, wealth, and luxury.

Echinacea

Use this plant in tea to keep your body guarded against flu and infections. Echinacea strengthens the immune system and keeps your body healthy and infection free.

Correspondences for Echinacea

Echinacea has the power to strengthen spell work, charms, and mojo bags, especially if it relates to healing and abundance. This flower is an ally in crown magic and clairvoyant protection.

Elderberries

Elderberries strengthen the immune system and are packed with antioxidants that can help heal and repair the body while fighting off illnesses, helping you to combat cold and flu season.

Correspondences for Elderberries

Elderberries are excellent for protection, healing, and blessings. This berry is beneficial in all healing teas.

Fennel

Fennel helps to regulate blood pressure, reduce water retention, and reduce bloating, constipation, and IBS symptoms. Fennel is excellent for skin care and will help heal acne.

Correspondences for Fennel

Fennel helps protect the home and body, and aids in mental strength to help you accomplish your goals.

Ginger

Ginger is an anti-inflammatory that helps to alleviate pain. Ginger also reduces nausea and helps to break down mucus to improve lung health and circulation.

Correspondences for Ginger

Ginger is known to speed things up, such as bringing a lover to you right away, bringing fast luck and quick cash. Ginger is fiery and will add power to your meditations and insights.

Ginkgo Biloba

Ginkgo biloba relieves anxiety and vertigo. It also helps concentration and builds memory strength.

Correspondences for Ginkgo Biloba

Ginkgo is ideal for sustaining a long, healthy life and aids in longevity work. This tree and her leaves aid in the protection of your health, wisdom, and family. Gingko is sometimes referred to as the tree of life.

Ginseng

Ginseng is an aphrodisiac and mild stimulant. This herb boosts your immune system and aids in fertility and male stamina.

Correspondences for Ginseng

Ginseng is used for love, wishes, beauty, and lust. This herb has been said to attract love and guard one's health, bringing money and producing passionate business deals.

Green Tea

Green tea is now grown in many countries but of course, like all teas, it was first grown in China. Green tea creates enhanced focus, and is rich in antioxidants, making it an ideal tea for promoting vitality, and alertness. It is an anti-inflammatory, boosts metabolism, improves brain function, regulates dopamine, and has been linked to helping reduce the risk of stroke and heart failure.

Green tea has more caffeine than white tea. It has a crisp flavor with hints of earthy and buttery flavors. There are also undertones of grassy freshness. This tea can become bitter if steeped too long.

Correspondences for Green Tea

Health, luck, love, prosperity, clear focus, deep connection to your body, mind, and spirit, making it a beneficial tea to drink before meditation, as it enhances long periods of focus. It is a superior focus tea for meditation, good health, and general well-being. Green tea also builds and strengthens your will. Using green tea leaves in a mojo bag can act as a protection of health.

Hemp Leaves

This is the cousin to cannabis. Hemp leaves contain cannabidiol, which has been shown to improve circulation in the body, bring down swelling, and aid in pain relief. Also known to ease panic attacks and help to calm the nervous system. This is an excellent tea for meditation and quiet thoughts.

Correspondences for Hemp Leaves

Hemp is used in magical practices to honor the Divine and communicate with other side. Hemp leaves are said to increase psychic awareness.

Hibiscus

Hibiscus is refreshing, as this is an excellent flower that brings a tart kick. This flower has been helpful in lowering sugar cravings and helping to slow and eliminate the conversion of carbs into sugar that can be stored as fat, making this flower helpful in weight management.

Correspondences for Hibiscus

Hibiscus can be used for love spells, dream magic, and beauty potions.

Holy Basil / Tulsi

Holy basil strengthens the immune system and is an anti-inflammatory which can bring down swelling and pain. It also has an uplifting quality and can aid in meditation by bringing a calm and relaxed state of well-being.

Correspondences for Holy Basil / Tulsi

Holy basil is ideal for meditation, prayer, and sacred offerings. This herb helps to balance body, mind, and spirit and has been known to ward off evil and keep you safe from harm.

Honeybush

Honeybush is an herb that is sweet and earthy in taste and can help to bring down sugar cravings by giving your teas an uplifting sweetness. Packed with antioxidants, this herb also brings with it the health benefits of being an immune booster.

Correspondences for Honeybush

Honeybush represents beauty, kindness, friendship, and loyalty. This herb is said to aid in weight loss by helping to reduce the cravings for sugar and junk food.

Horny Goat Weed

Horny goat weed increases blood flow. This flowering plant is believed to stimulate male and female hormones to improve sexual function and arousal.

Correspondences for Horny Goat Weed

Horny goat weed is useful when your intentions and desires are for all things love, passion, sex, lust, desire, drive, and ambition, and serves as an ignitor of the seminal spark.

Jasmine Flower

Jasmine flower protects brain function and oral health. It can act as a sedative and mood stabilizer, making this flower helpful to a woman's reproductive system, calming the body and the mind, as well as stabilizing mood swings.

Correspondences for Jasmine Flower

Jasmine flower can be used for beauty, love, longevity, and a long, healthy life. This flower is said to call the Fae folk when you wish to seek a favor.

Jasmine Tea

With origins in China, jasmine tea can be any variety of tea that has been infused with the essence of the jasmine flower. It is most commonly used with green tea. Jasmine tea has an extraordinary scent and healing properties of its aromatherapy benefits serve as a mood balancer. This tea also helps lift depression, aids in the relief of menopause symptoms, and brings tranquility and relaxation.

Correspondences for Jasmine Tea

Jasmine tea is said to give long life and longevity. It brings beauty to those who wear it and drink it. Jasmine is also known to summon the Fae folk.

Kava Kava

Kava kava can help with anxiety stress, insomnia, and body stiffness. This root can aid in the calming of sore, aching, or stiff joints, and muscle spasms.

Correspondences for Kava Kava

The kava kava root is hypnotic and can aid in vision quests. It is also known to bring protection when on vision quest journeys.

Lapsang Souchong Tea

Lapsang souchong tea is a full caffeine black tea that is dried over woo burning fires. This process gives the tea a robust and smoky sensation. This a full-bodied tea with deep undertones of forest and flame.

Correspondences for Lapsang Souchong Tea

Lapsang souchong tea is known to bring balance and peace to war. This is often attributed to how it brings warmth and fire into the body, allowing you to become one with fire and tea.

Lavender

Lavender is useful for treating anxiety, insomnia, depression, and restlessness. It makes a delicious and hypnotic scent that can be drank in tea or used in aromatherapy meditation.

Correspondences for Lavender

Uses for lavender include helping with meditation, love spells, happiness, and calming an angry spouse, and soothing crying children.

Lemon Balm

Lemon balm is related to the mint family. It may boost cognitive thinking, ease stress, improve mood, and help fight fatigue.

Correspondences for Lemon Balm

Lemon balm is useful in bringing love, keeps a lover faithful, and brings renewed happiness to stale relationships.

Lemongrass

Lemongrass helps to reduce fever, anxiety, stress, and depression. This herb is also known to steady blood pressure, balance your immune system, and combat infections. Lemongrass may also boost cognitive thinking and memory skills.

Correspondences for Lemongrass

Lemongrass repels snakes and psychic attacks. It can also be used to enhance meditation and increase psychic awareness.

Lemon Verbena

Lemon Verbena has been used throughout history to stop muscle spasms and act as a mild sedative, helping to calm down manic thoughts and limit irritability.

Correspondences for Lemon Verbena

Lemon verbena clears away negativity and aids in glamour work and beauty spells. It is also useful for protection of success and personal power.

Licorice Root

Licorice root soothes sore throats and eases stomach pain, gas, and diarrhea, helping to maintain a balanced gut.

Correspondences for Licorice Root

Licorice root promotes fidelity. This root can also help you direct your focused attention on keeping your prosperity and money safe.

Mango

Mango is beneficial in managing diabetes and helping your respiratory system. It is also high in vitamins, providing an extra boost to the health of your immune system.

Correspondences for Mango

Mango is ideal for fostering love, happiness, harmony, marriage, and romance. Mango tea also aids in inspiration and mood elevation.

Matcha Tea

Matcha is a green tea that has been ground down to a fine bright green powder. The powder is then whisked into hot water until it creates a frothy broth. Of all the teas, matcha is highest in antioxidants because the tea is ground so finely. Because of this, matcha tea makes its way directly into your bloodstream, helping to boost your energy, focus, and overall wellness.

Correspondences for Matcha Tea

Matcha tea's correspondences range from the spiritual to the physical. For instance, matcha has been known for centuries to help with inducing trance-like states in deep meditation, as it was originally used for this purpose by Buddhist monks. Matcha delivers great benefits to your health, promoting vitality and strength. It is also applied to magical practices and ceremonies for manifesting prosperity.

Mugwort

The mugwort herb is considered helpful as a sleep aid, stress reducer, and anxiety calmer, and can aid in digestion and internal health.

Note: You should never use mugwort when pregnant or if you are trying to become pregnant. This herb can bring on the menstruation cycle by weakening the lining of the womb. In medieval times, mugwort tea was used as a natural birth control and has been known to cause the body to abort early pregnancies. It is highly advised not to use this herb while pregnant or while breast feeding.

Correspondences for Mugwort

Mugwort is associated with the moon because this herb helps to promote deep sleep that is associated with R.E.M (rapid eye movement) which occurs when dreaming. Mugwort is also known to cause lucid dreaming and astral travel.

Nettles

Nettles reduces water retention and bloating, which helps to flush toxins from the body, liver, and kidneys. It also aids in relieving arthritis and muscle pain.

Correspondences for Nettles

Nettles is ideal to use for protection and safety of family. Nettles sends back the evil eye and breaks curses and hexes. It is also used to metaphorically sting your enemy.

Nutmeg

Nutmeg can help relieve pain, soothe indigestion, strengthen cognitive function, detoxify the body, boost skin health, alleviate oral conditions, reduce insomnia, increase immune system function, and improve blood circulation.

Correspondences for Nutmeg

Nutmeg is ideal for boosting confidence, improving comfortability in social interactions, fidelity, and kindness. Nutmeg is also good at facilitating emotional openness and revealing past lives. It has been said that nutmeg can boost the luck of a gambler.

Oolong Tea

Oolong tea is a tea that has been processed at the halfway point between green tea and black tea. This allows the tea to retain a higher number of green benefits, while also providing a richer, smoother flavor of a black tea. The flavor of oolong tea is full bodied and ranges from a toasty richness to earthy, nutty, and sometimes sweet undertones.

Known for promoting heart health, dental health, and skin health, oolong tea will keep you energized and focused, helping to create a productive day.

Correspondences for Oolong Tea

Correspondences for oolong tea include love, reflection, emotional balance, inner peace, and spiritual well-being. Because oolong is processed right between green tea and black tea stages, it lends itself to be a facilitator of balance, as it keeps you energized and focused, but also producing a sense of calm.

For these reasons and more, there are many beneficial uses for oolong tea that include divination, meditation and balanced thinking, and brings deep reflection on relationships and matters of the heart. Using oolong tea in love amulets strengthens the attractions.

Oolong is also regarded as a great promoter of truth. An old wives' tale claims that drinking oolong with your guest will reveal truths and may act as a truth serum in some situations.

Papaya

Papaya is a fruit that can help heal the internal workings of your gut. It aids in balancing and relieving gas and indigestion. Papaya contains a natural enzyme, papain, that helps to break down excess proteins in the stomach, making digestion easier.

Correspondences for Papaya

Papaya is useful for protection of health of the body. It is also known to bring success in competition and battle.

Parsley

Parsley can help with kidney function, promote healthy blood pressure, and regulate menstrual cycles.

Correspondences for Parsley

Uses for parsley include domestic tranquility, energy, luck, and protection of the home and auto from accidents.

Peaches

Peaches are high in vitamin C, and thus, they help to keep the immune system strong and aid in healing flesh wounds and injuries. Peaches help protect your skin and hair against free radicals and pollutants. This beautiful fruit can also help clear up acne.

Correspondences for Peaches

Peaches are useful for achieving longevity, protection, and vitality in your life. Peaches are also said to increase the desire for sexual intercourse.

Pennyroyal

Related to the mint family, pennyroyal helps regulate the female reproductive system. This herb should never be used if you are pregnant or wanting to be pregnant.

Correspondences for Pennyroyal

Pennyroyal is useful for protection and often used in casting charms. When sprinkled or planted around the home, pennyroyal is said to ward off pests. This correspondence is probably due to its strong mint aroma that pests naturally avoid.

Peppermint

Peppermint relieves nausea, anxiety, and indigestion. Peppermint can help relieve the symptoms brought on by a common cold such as coughs, stuffy nose, and congestion. Peppermint can also open the airways to your lungs and help you breathe deeper. Peppermint is known to relax the nerves and is excellent for mental focus.

Correspondences for Peppermint

Peppermint is ideal for wealth attraction, money, and prosperity. Peppermint is said to bring good business and business partners. This herb also helps to center and balance chaotic and racing thoughts in the mind.

Another useful correspondence for peppermint is that when planted around the home, this herb will ward off pests such as mice, fleas, ticks, and spiders. You can also sprinkle dried peppermint leaves around the home for the same effect; however, this method might only be temporary.

Pomegranate

Pomegranates are loaded with beneficial nutrients that can help increase oxygen flow to your body. It also helps to combat cancer causing free radicals that damage skin and internal organs.

Correspondences for Pomegranate

Pomegranate is a highly regarded sacred fruit and juice, where its beneficial correspondences can be found in many myths and traditions. This fruit is helpful when beginning dangerous journeys and soul-searching work and inner meditation. Pomegranate is powerfully feminine and may be used to call goddesses to your aid for guidance.

Pu-erh Tea

Pu-erh tea is double fermented and holds bold flavors. It is rich in color and tannins. Pu-erh tea is steamed and aged. The longer it has aged, the more sought-after the tea. Some of the most expensive teas in the world are pu-erh tea, due to the year of the crop, the storage of the tea, and the length of years it has been stored.

Akin to wine, pu-erh ages well, and over time its deep, rich, and earth flavors are enhanced. The taste is heavier than all other tea counterparts, with strong earth, deep molasses, spicy, and chocolaty notes bringing pu-erh teas to full-rounded finish. Contains caffeine similar to black tea levels.

Correspondences for Pu-erh Tea

Clarity, alertness, romance, and wisdom. This tea is also useful when working on memory recall and is used to understand family history. For this reason, pu-erh is an aid when blending past and future together.

Pu-erh is known to offer a myriad of health benefits, including increased stamina and fortitude. It also helps with diabetes and high cholesterol, and lends to increased stamina and fortitude.

Raspberry Leaf

Raspberry leaf is high in vitamins such as B, A, C, and E, and minerals such as potassium, magnesium, and calcium. These are helpful in relieving symptoms of P.M.S., endometriosis, and menopause by balancing your hormones.

Correspondences for Raspberry Leaf

Uses for raspberry leaf include nurturing, love, family, fertility, and the protection and healing of women.

Red Clover

Red clover can be used to ease the symptoms of menopause by aiding in the reduction of hot flashes, soothing sore breasts, and balancing hormones.

Correspondences for Red Clover

Uses for red clover include good luck, protection, happiness, joy, and protection of friendships. Red clover is also said to attract the Fae folk.

Rooibos

Rooibos is high in antioxidants helping to keep your body and your internal organs strong. This tea is beneficial for keeping your blood healthy.

Correspondences for Rooibos

Rooibos's rich red color makes it ideal for love, passion, and desire spells. This tea can aid in healing damaged blood lines and generational disfunction.

When brewed strong to release its color, this tea can be used as a representative of blood, in place of blood, if a spell calls for blood.

Rose Hips

Rose hips are high in vitamin C. This part of the rose is known to boost your immune system and has been called a superfood, which can aid in brain function and total well-being.

Correspondences for Rose Hips

Rose hips are ideal for inspiring love and beauty. Rose hips also bring luck, laughter, and healing.

Rose Petals (red)

Rose petals help facilitate healthy glowing skin, reduce menstrual irritations, and help balance mood swings.

Correspondences for Rose Petals

Red rose petals symbolize love and passion. Roses soften negativity and heal matters of the heart. Red rose petals are ideal for love teas, potions, and love spells.

Rosemary

Rosemary clears mental fog and helps you focus and protects your vision. It also increases brain function and helps to get rid of headaches and migraines. Rosemary helps clear breathing passages that can aid in the relief of asthma.

Correspondences for Rosemary

Rosemary is useful in cleansing, purification, healing, and removal of obstacles and mental blocks. This plant brings protection when planted near the entry way of your property or office.

Sarsaparilla

Sarsaparilla has been used to treat flu-like symptoms, aid in the healing of irritated and inflamed skin, and benefit those who suffer from psoriasis.

Correspondences for Sarsaparilla

Sarsaparilla is ideal for promoting overall good health. It can also be used to bring happiness to an unhappy family or friendship. For this reason, the sarsaparilla root is useful in bringing people together in harmonious reunions and celebrations.

Spearmint

Spearmint promotes healthy memory and focus, aids in digestion, and helps stomach aches. Spearmint is also helpful in balancing your emotions and hormones. It is excellent for opening airways in the lungs to promote deeper breathing.

Correspondences for Spearmint

Uses for spearmint include its help in promoting wealth and prosperity and attracting money. It is also ideal for sharpening your mental focus during meditation and spell work.

Stevia Leaf

The stevia leaf is intensely sweet and can help bring down sugar cravings, and in turn, it aids in bringing down high blood sugar. Stevia is also beneficial to those with diabetes, and to those who have a sweet tooth and are seeking to curb their sugar cravings.

Correspondences for Stevia Leaf

Stevia leaves aid in working with Fae magic. Stevia is also used in trickery spells and for secret keeping.

Valerian Root

Valerian root, which is also known as the natural "valium," is ideal as a sleep aid and insomnia reducer. Although this is a smelly root, it is said to be helpful in easing headaches, anxiety, and nervousness.

Correspondences for Valerian Root

Valerian root is great for dream work and shadow self-exploration. This root is said to aid in creating a trance-like state for meditation and scrying.

Vanilla Bean

Vanilla bean is an exotic fruit that comes from the vanilla orchid. It has been used in medicines and tinctures to enhance flavor and to bring a calmness and pleasant feeling that helps to facilitate healing and overall good health. Vanilla bean can also be helpful as an antacid, relieving indigestion,and heartburn.

Correspondences for Vanilla Bean

Vanilla bean is useful in bringing a calm, nurturing aspect to your life. Vanilla bean brings a sweetness to love and encourages maternal healing. Vanilla bean also holds power of love, and divine feminine healing, which is beneficial for women, men, and children.

White Tea

White tea, which is sometimes called silver tips, is known for bringing joy, clear focus, clarity, enhancement of health, and emotional healing. It is also excellent for renewing skin and hair, delivering a healthy shine. White tea is a superior clear-thinking tea for meditation and prayer, which is why it is ideal for purifying your thoughts and actions and bringing blessings and protection.

Correspondences for White Tea

White tea ienhances psychic ability and aids in aura cleansing, chakra balancing, clear thinking, and connecting to the Divine, spirits, and deities. Using white tea to cleanse magical tools helps to neutralize negativity and balance the tools' proper energy. You can also burn the leaves as an offering to deities and loved ones who have crossed over.

Wormwood

Wormwood can be used to reduce fever and helps to cleanse the liver. It also uplifts depression, soothes muscle pain, reduces memory loss, and can cleanse the guts of worm and parasite infections.

Note: This herb is the main ingredient in absinth. Absinth was known as the "Green Fairy" in the mid-nineteenth century. This was an avant-garde drink amongst artistic crowds searching for more inspiration than getting tipsy. It also contains thujone, which in high doses is a nerve toxin and can cause mild to extreme hallucinations. It is also worth noting that the drink and its original recipe are illegal in most countries.

Correspondences for Wormwood

Wormwood is helpful for divination and to increase psychic abilities. When applied to your tea, wormwood promotes astral travel and lucid dreaming.

Yellow Tea

Yellow tea is low in acid and tannins and is therefore easy on sensitive tummies. With a low caffeine level, yellow tea is not as overpowering as black tea or green tea but is up quite lifting. Yellow tea is light in flavor, leaning to a slight vegetal taste, sometimes with citrus and earthy undertones.

Correspondences for Yellow Tea

Correspondences for yellow tea include happiness, prosperity, abundance, and health, which is why it is a wonderful tea for meditating on wellness and abundance. With its mild and crisp flavor profile, as well as being low in acid and tannin, yellow tea easy on sensitive tummies.

Yerba Maté

Yerba maté can boost your metabolism and assist you in burning belly fat. It is also known to create physical energy and aid in overall wellness. Yerba maté has been known to help keep you focused and alert.

Correspondences for Yerba Maté

Yerba maté is useful for boosting your confidence and courage. Yerba maté is also a good drink that facilitates your inner drive and ambition, both physically and mentally.

Appendix B
Additional Tea Recipes

Here are some additional recipes, helpful hints, and good old-fashioned folk remedies to add to your own apothecary.

Good Night Tea

This tea blend and personal ritual is to help your mind find calm and peace to allow you to slip into a restful sleep that can induce relaxation and restfulness.

This tea is extra helpful when prepared with water charged by the new moon. This moon energy is perfect for the internal quest of sleep.

Gather your ingredients and brew yourself a nice strong cup. This cup of tea should be consumed about an hour before bedtime. I recommend that when you are preparing for bed, and taking in Good Night Tea, to stay off electronic devices in this hour, including television.

To occupy your mind, I suggest reading or simply trying to meditate about what you would like to dream about while you drink your tea. Meditate on how it will feel in the morning after a good night's sleep. Visualize how rested you will feel, and how productive your day will be.

When lying down to sleep, be sure to remind yourself that you are ready to sleep deeply and peacefully. Tell yourself that you will awake refreshed and energized from all the restful sleep you get.

Here is what you'll need:

> ½ cup dried peppermint leaves. Peppermint helps relieve tension.
>
> ¼ cup dried catnip leaves. Catnip helps relax your mind and promote sleep. This herb makes cats crazy and humans lazy.
>
> 2 tablespoons chamomile. Chamomile helps calm your mind and relax your body.
>
> 2 teaspoons lavender. Lavender helps to induce restful sleep.
>
> 3 teaspoons red rose petals. Rose petals help to calm anxiety and relax the mind.

This tea recipe will yield at least fifteen to eighteen pots of tea. Store remainder in an airtight container out of direct sunlight to preserve the quality of the herbs and the freshness of the blend, and to prolong the shelf life.

Inspiration and Joy Tea

The Inspiration and Joy Tea blend is helpful when you are beginning a new project or are working on creative ideas. This tea is uplifting and can make a difference in your attitude if you drink it at work or home, especially if you are unhappy there. Remember to brew it with a clear mental picture of the feeling of joy and inspiration you are seeking.

Here is what you'll need:

> ½ cup of green tea. Green tea brings you focus and a boost of energy.
>
> ¼ cup of lemon peels. Lemon peels bring happiness and help clear away negativity.
>
> 2 tablespoons of lemongrass. Lemongrass boosts cognitive thinking and memory. It also wards off psychic attacks.

Brew 1 to 2 teaspoons per cup, depending on your preferable strength and likes.

This Inspiration and Joy Tea recipe will yield at least fifteen to eighteen pots of tea. Store remainder in an airtight container out of direct sunlight to preserve the quality of the herbs and the freshness of the blend, and to prolong the shelf life.

Dream Journey Tea

This deep sleeping Dream Journey Tea will aid in creating vivid dreams. This tea is known to help facilitate astral projection and lucid dreaming. It is recommended to keep a journal by your bedside to write down your dream experiences, so you do not forget them during the day.

The Dream Journey Tea should be used with caution. For example, if you are pregnant or wanting to become pregnant, do not use this tea recipe.

Here is what you'll need:

¼ cup peppermint. Peppermint relaxes the mind and readies it for sleep.

2 tablespoons catnip. Catnip helps you get to sleep.

1 tablespoon kava kava. Kava kava calms the mind and relaxes the body.

1 tablespoon mugwort. Mugwort aids in lucid dreaming and astral projection.

1 tablespoon wormwood. Wormwood aids in lucid dreaming and astral projection.

1 teaspoon lavender flowers. Lavender helps to induce restful and peaceful sleep.

1 teaspoon stevia leaves (optional). Stevia is an herb that adds sweetness to balance the bitterness from the mugwort and wormwood. Stevia leaves will symbolically bring sweetness to your dream journey.

The recipe for your dream journey tea will yield at least five pots of tea. Store remainder in an airtight container out of direct sunlight to preserve the quality of the herbs and the freshness of the blend, and to prolong the shelf life.

Sniffle Mint Tea

This tea is to help reduce the length and effect of the common cold. It is an easy-to-acquire blend because the botanicals are common and easy to find.

Here is what you'll need:

¼ cup peppermint tea

2 tablespoons chamomile

1 tablespoon dried licorice root (chopped)

1 tablespoon dried chopped ginger (This can be substituted for grated fresh ginger if making it on the spot.)

2 teaspoons whole rosemary leaves

Honey to taste can be added when brewed. Honey is beneficial in soothing sore throats and calming persistent coughs.

Brew as needed for common cold ailments. Store in an airtight container out of direct sunlight to preserve the quality of the herbs and the freshness of the blend, and to prolong the shelf life.

Bibliography

Andrews, Ted. *Crystal Balls and Crystal Bowls*. St. Paul, MN: Llewellyn Publications, 1999.

Baum, Isadora. "These Hibiscus Tea Health Benefits May Have You Trading in Your Daily Chai." *Oprah Magazine*, March 11, 2019. https://www.oprahmag.com/life/health/a26785615/health-benefits-of-hibiscus-tea/.

Cunningfolk, Alexis J. "The Twelve Paths of Healing." Worts and Cunning. Accessed September 24, 2021. http://www.wortsandcunning.com/blog/2015/3/30/12-paths-of-healing-astroherbology.

Cunningham, Scott. *Encyclopedia of Magical Herbs*. St. Paul, MN: Llewellyn Worldwide, 1992.

Dow, Caroline. *Tea Leaf Reading for Beginners*. Woodbury, MN: Llewellyn Worldwide, 2019.

Dresden, Danielle. "What's the Difference Between Cannabis CBD and Hemp CBD?" Medical News Today. Accessed on September 24, 2021. https://www.medicalnewstoday.com/articles/hemp-cbd-vs-cannabis-cbd.

Emoto, Dr. Masaru. *The Hidden Messages in Water*. Hillsboro, OR: Beyond Words Publishing, 2004.

"Five Facts About Nostradamus That You Probably Didn't Know and Ten Events About the World That He Knew All Too Well." India Today. Accessed September 24, 2021. https://www.indiatoday.in/education-today/gk

-current-affairs/story/nostradamus-facts-and-predictions-1022000-2017
-07-02.

Gonzales, Carolina. "Sacred Intention." *Witches and Pagans* 37 (2019): 11–15.

Gunnars, Kris. "Ten Evidence-based Benefits of Green Tea." Health Line. Accessed September 24, 2021. https://www.healthline.com/nutrition/top-10
-evidence-based-health-benefits-of-green-tea.

Hall, Judy. *The Crystal Bible*. Toronto: Walking Stick Press, 2003.

Hartley, Louise, Nadine Flowers, Jennifer Holmes, Aileen Clarke, Saverio
Stranges, Lee Hooper, and Karen Rees. "Green and Black Tea for the Primary Prevention of Cardiovascular Disease." *Cochrane Database of Systematic Reviews* 6 (2013): CD009934. https://doi.org/10.1002/14651858
.CD009934.pub2.

Heiss, Mary Lou, and Robert J. Heiss. *The Tea Enthusiast Handbook*. Berkley,
CA: Ten Speed Press, 2010.

Hinchliffe, Sandra. *High Tea: Gracious Cannabis Tea-Time Recipes for Every Occasion*. New York: Skyhorse, 2017.

"History of Marijuana as Medicine: 2900 BC to Present." BrittanicaProCon.
Accessed September 24, 2021. https://medicalmarijuana.procon.org
/historical-timeline/.

Hogue, John. *Nostradamus and the Millennium: Predictions of the Future*. New
York: Doubleday, 1987.

"Iced Tea History." What's Cooking America. Accessed September 23, 2021.
https://whatscookingamerica.net/history/icedteahistory.htm.

Illes, Judika. *The Element Encyclopedia of 5,000 Spells*. New York: HarperCollins,
2004.

Kandola, Aaron. "Does Green Tea Help Weight Loss?" Medical News Today.
Accessed September 23, 2021. https://www.medicalnewstoday.com
/articles/320540.

Kennedy, Ann. *Aromatherapy for Beginners*. Dallas, TX: Althea Press, 2018.

Klipopmekaar, Richard. "The History of Rooibos Tea." Klipopmekarr. Accessed
September 23, 2021. https://www.klipopmekaar.co.za/rooibos-tea-history/.

Low Dog, Tieraona. "Healing Remedies: A Holistic Approach to Healing and Wellness." *National Geographic*, 2018.

Mankey, Jason. *The Witch's Book of Shadows*. Woodbury, MN: Llewellyn Worldwide, 2017.

"Marijuana." History.com. Accessed September 24, 2021. https://www.history .com/topics/crime/history-of-marijuana#section_1.

McGarvie, Irene. *Mirror Gazing*. Ontario: Ancient Wisdom, 2010.

Nagdeve, Meenakshi. "Ten Best Benefits of Bergamot Oil." OrganicFacts. Accessed September 24, 2021. https://www.organicfacts.net/health-benefits /essential-oils/health-benefits-of-bergamot-essential-oil.html.

Ody, Penelope. *The Complete Medicinal Herbal*. London: DK Publishing, 1993.

Ohisi, Tomokazan, Shingo Goto, Pervin Monira, Mamouru Isemura, and Yoriyuki Nakamura. "Anti-inflammatory Actions of Green Tea." *Anti-inflammatory Anti-allergy Agents in Medicinal Chemistry* 15, no. 2 (2016): 74–90. https://doi.org/ 10.2174/1871523015666160915154443.

Paddock, Catherine, PhD. "Does a Cup of Tea Reduce Stress?" Medical News Today. Accessed September 24, 2021. https://www.medicalnewstoday.com /articles/160668#1.

Pettigrew, Jane, and Bruce Richardson. *The New Tea Companion*. Amsterdam: Benjamin Press, 2018.

Pettigrew, Jane. *A Social History of Tea*. London: The National Trust, 2001.

"Plants and Herbs for your Zodiac Sign." Tarot.com. Accessed September 24, 2021. https://www.tarot.com/astrology/plants-herbs-zodiac-sign.

Richardson, Bruce. "Boston Tea Party Ships and Museum." Boston Tea Party Ships and Museum. Accessed September 23, 2021. https://www .bostonteapartyship.com/tea-blog/who-invented-the-teabag.

Rister, Robert. *Herbal Medicine*. New York: Avery Publishing Group, 1999.

Robbins, Shawn, and Charity Bedell. *The Good Witch's Guide*. New York: Sterling Ethos, 2017.

Rose, Sara. *For All the Tea in China*. London: Penguin, 2010.

Sobell, Dava. "The Resurrection of Nostradamus." *Omni* 16, no. 3 (December 1993): 42. https://link.gale.com/apps/doc/A14607996 /AONE?u=anon~864c79ec&sid=googleScholar&xid=e474dbc0.

Standage, Tom. *A History of the World in 6 Glasses*. New York: Bloomsbury, 2005.

"Tea and Cancer Prevention." National Cancer Institute. Accessed September 23, 2021. https://www.cancer.gov/cancertopics/causes-prevention/risk/diet /tea-fact-sheet.

Telesco, Patricia. *A Witch's Beverages and Brews*. Frisco, CO: Career Press, 2001.

———. *Kitchen Witches Guide to Brews and Potions*. Frisco, CO: New Page, 2005.

Tyson, Donald. *Scrying for Beginners*. Woodbury, MN: Llewellyn Worldwide, 1997.

Venables, Michelle C., Carl J. Hulston, Hannah R. Cox, and Asker E. Jeukendrup. "Green Tea Extract Ingestion, Fat Oxidation, and Glucose Tolerance in Healthy Humans." *The American Journal of Clinical Nutrition* 87, no. 3 (2008): 778–84. https://doi.org/10.1093/ajcn/87.3.778.

Ware, Megan, RND. "What Are the Benefits of Green Tea?" Medical News Today. Accessed September 23, 2021. https://www.medicalnewstoday.com /articles/269538#health-benefits.

Warner, Jennifer. "Drinking Black Tea May Soothe Stress." WebMD. Accessed September 24, 2021. https://www.webmd.com/food-recipes /news/20061005/drinking-black-tea-may-soothe-stress.

"Water Facts." US Bureau of Reclamation. Accessed September 24, 2021. https://www.usbr.gov/mp/arwec/water-facts-ww-water-sup.html.

"Water Safe Crystals: Which Ones Are and Which Are Not?" Amarisland. Accessed September 24, 2021. https://amarisland.myshopify.com/blogs/news /water-safe-crystals-which-ones-are-and-which-are-not.

Wilson, Natalie. "Keeping Old Herbal Alive." *Witch Way Magazine: The Herbal Guide* Volume 3, 2018.

Wilson, Natalie. "Of Herbs and Practical Magic." *Witch Way Magazine: The Herbal Guide Volume 2,* 2017.

"Your Ideal Tea Based on Your Zodiac Sign." David's Tea. Accessed September 24, 2021. http://blog.davidstea.com/en/your-ideal-tea-based-on-your -zodiac-sign/.

Zak, Victoria. *20,000 Secrets of Tea.* New York: Dell, 1999.

Zielinski, Eric. "Nine Benefits of Bergamot Essential Oil." Natural Living Family. Accessed September 24, 2021. https://naturallivingfamily.com/9 -benefits-of-bergamot-essential-oil/.

To Write to the Author

If you wish to contact the author or would like more information about this book, please write to the author in care of Llewellyn Worldwide Ltd. and we will forward your request. Both the author and the publisher appreciate hearing from you and learning of your enjoyment of this book and how it has helped you. Llewellyn Worldwide Ltd. cannot guarantee that every letter written to the author will be answered, but all will be forwarded. Please write to:

Jenay Marontate
℅ Llewellyn Worldwide
2143 Wooddale Drive
Woodbury, MN 55125-2989

Please enclose a self-addressed stamped envelope for reply,
or $1.00 to cover costs. If outside the U.S.A., enclose
an international postal reply coupon.

Many of Llewellyn's authors have websites with additional information and resources. For more information, please visit our website at http://www.llewellyn.com.